Masterful Leadership

Wisdom They Don't Teach in Business School

Michael E. Rindler
Jack H. Mitstifer, MD

ISBN: 978-0-615-87012-6

Dedication

Masterful Leadership is dedicated to all healthcare leaders. We have great admiration for supervisors, department directors, nurse managers, vice presidents, physician leaders, chief financial officers, chief operating officers, chief executives, and governing board members. These leaders run the nation's healthcare systems, hospitals, clinics, physician offices, and outpatient centers. They strive and succeed in delivering the best clinical care and the best customer service to patients and their families.

We have been profoundly fortunate to work with a number of fine leaders and role models. We are grateful for the opportunity to know and to learn from these wonderful leaders:

Craig Babbitt	Wally Miller, Sr., MD
Paula Bauer, MD	Sister Mary Mollison
Beverly Bokovitz, RN	Shawn Molsberger
Jack Bradford, DO	William Moore
Les Donahue	Jeff Myers
Frank Douglas, MD	Diane Patrick, RN
Sister Kathryn Easley	Rhonda Perry
Donald Faulk	Leroy Rheault
Alan Friggy, MD	William Richardson
Satoshi Furukawa, MD	Stephen Ronstrom
James Gardner	Jack Samsel
Michael Guthrie, MD	Dan Schelble, MD
David Hannan	Tim Stover, MD
William Hebble, MD	Quint Studer
Sister Marilyn Kuzmickus	Richard Umbdenstock
George Litman, MD	Thomas Whelan

This book aspires to affirm the good work that healthcare leaders do every day and offers ideas to make their work as leaders more effective and their organizations more successful.

Michael E. Rindler
Jack H. Mitstifer, MD

Other Titles by Michael E. Rindler

Strategic Cost Reduction: Leading Your Hospital to Success

The Essential Guide to Managing Consultants:
Strategies for Healthcare Leaders

The Challenge of Hospital Governance:
How to Become an Exemplary Board

Managing a Hospital Turnaround:
From Crisis to Profitability in Three Challenging Years

Putting Patients and Profits into Perspective:
The Right Kind of Leadership Produces the Best Patient Outcomes

Masterful Leadership
Wisdom They Don't Teach in Business School

FOREWORD   iii

INTRODUCTION: ESSENCE OF MASTERFUL LEADERSHIP   v

COMMUNICATION IN LEADERSHIP   1

Chapter 1	Listening	3
Chapter 2	Connecting with Patients	5
Chapter 3	Connecting with Staff	7
Chapter 4	Meetings	9
Chapter 5	Presentations	11
Chapter 6	Continuous Updating	13
Chapter 7	A Touch of Humanity	15
Chapter 8	Confidentiality and Trust	17

PRACTICING LEADERSHIP   19

Chapter 9	Working Knowledge	21
Chapter 10	Setting Expectations	23
Chapter 11	Accountability	25
Chapter 12	Consistency Is Good, Complacency Is Bad	27
Chapter 13	Effective Subordinate Skills	29
Chapter 14	Situational Awareness	31
Chapter 15	Making Decisions	33
Chapter 16	Planning	35

PEOPLE LEADERSHIP   37

Chapter 17	Hiring	39
Chapter 18	Teaching and Mentoring	41
Chapter 19	Evaluating	43
Chapter 20	Firing	45
Chapter 21	Number Two	47
Chapter 22	Direct Reports	49
Chapter 23	Micro- and Macromanagement	51
Chapter 24	Setting an Exemplary Example	53
Chapter 25	Trusted Advisors	55

PHYSICIANS IN LEADERSHIP   57

    Chapter 26   Engaging the Medical Staff   59
    Chapter 27   Unique Benefits of Physician Leaders   61
    Chapter 28   New Leadership Models   63
    Chapter 29   Recruiting Physician Leaders   65
    Chapter 30   Mentoring Physician Leaders   67
    Chapter 31   Pitfalls for Physician Leaders   69
    Chapter 32   Balance as a Physician Leader   71

VALUES IN LEADERSHIP   73

    Chapter 33   Moral Compass   75
    Chapter 34   Courage   77
    Chapter 35   Power   79
    Chapter 36   Effort vs. Outcome   81
    Chapter 37   Bad Behavior   83
    Chapter 38   Never Mess with the Help   85
    Chapter 39   Work/Life Balance   87
    Chapter 40   Solitude   89

SYMBOLS OF LEADERSHIP   91

    Chapter 41   Executive Assistants   93
    Chapter 42   Office and Access   95
    Chapter 43   Good Manners   97
    Chapter 44   Taking Office   99
    Chapter 45   Leaving Office   101
    Chapter 46   Succession   103

THE MEANING OF MASTERFUL LEADERSHIP   105

    Chapter 47   What Masterful Leaders Never Do   107
    Chapter 48   Defining Moments   109
    Chapter 49   Measures of Success   111
    Chapter 50   What Masterful Leaders Always Do   113

Foreword

Very early in my healthcare career I got lucky. I came upon a book written by Michael Rindler, *Putting Patients and Profits Into Perspective*. As I read the book I used my yellow highlighter to mark those areas I wanted to review and a pen for underlining the most important parts and to write notes. Upon completing the book there were very few spots not highlighted or underlined, with many notes in the margins. The book was a career saver.

I had the same experience 25 years later reading *Masterful Leadership: Wisdom They Don't Teach in Business School*, by Michael Rindler and Jack Mitstifer, MD. In addition to being a great read, the book is user-friendly and provided in a cost-effective manner. It is evident the authors understand the healthcare delivery system. In reading the book, I had to bury my envy. I should have written this book. I wish I had written this book. Then reality set in. If I could have, I would have. The facts are I could not and did not. Fortunately for you, Michael and Jack did a much better job than I would have.

You will likely have many takeaways, affirmation that many of the decisions and actions you have taken were the correct ones. Most leaders are better than they give themselves credit for. Healthcare professionals are hard on themselves. The authors share lessons they have learned, many painfully learned. Wow! I am so glad I am reading this. I am gaining skills and wisdom that will help me be a better leader. Thus I will be able to achieve even better results for my organization and myself.

Over the years I have observed thousands of healthcare leaders. They tend to fall into two categories. One is those who tend to lean toward rationalization and excuses. The second is those who are solution-finders. Seeing you are about to read this book, you are in the second category. You are a solution seeker. By seeking, one finds.

Thank you to Michael and Jack for sharing such lessons, tips and wisdom. What a gift your book is to current and future healthcare leaders. Thank you to the readers. You are dedicated to making yourself better and your organizations better. Most importantly, you continue to make patient care better.

That is why healthcare professionals do what you do. You make a difference. Thank you.

Quint Studer
The Studer Group

Introduction: Essence of Masterful Leadership

The essence of masterful leadership is listening and learning. Masters of any endeavor listen intently and learn, with practice, to be the very best. We learn with equal measure from our successes, challenges, and failures. Our greatest hope is that this book will inspire healthcare leaders who are already good or great to endeavor to be masterful.

"Masterful" is the pinnacle of leadership skills, applied so as to achieve exceptional results. Masterful leaders are not born. They become masterful with experience and by gaining cumulative wisdom. They are superb listeners and lifelong learners. They have character and unshakable integrity.

Leadership is personal. Management theories, elegant organization charts, and well-crafted strategic plans do not guarantee an organization's success. Only people, doing their best work, led by the best leaders, guarantee success. Acquiring the skills and wisdom to be a masterful leader is a lifelong journey.

Masterful leadership thrives in diverse settings: from a single department in a community hospital to the CEO's office in a large multi-hospital healthcare system; from a small rural hospital to a medical residency program in a diversified teaching hospital. Masterful leadership is not defined by organization size, geography, or payer mix. It can be found anywhere, including your organization.

What follows are timeless leadership skills, values, and wisdom they don't teach in business school. All of these skills can be learned and emulated. That is the beauty of masterful leadership. It can be practiced and perfected. Make the journey. Become a masterful leader.

Notes to readers: Key points are contained in the box near the beginning of each chapter. Many chapters also contain a vignette box: true stories intended to illustrate the message of the chapter. For simplicity, "he" is used rather than the more cumbersome "he or she."

COMMUNICATION IN LEADERSHIP

Communication is the way leaders influence others. Mark Twain once mused, *"Everyone talks about the weather, but no one does anything about it."* So it goes with communication: lots of talk, little action. Leaders have a profound opportunity with communication. Personal communication is always best, even in an era of wonderful electronic options. An e-mail or text message has yet to inspire an organization or its people to greatness. One well-spent personal communication minute can do more than a hundred e-mails. It does not take great oratory skills to communicate. It takes the desire and willingness to connect. Connecting starts with listening, the most powerful communication tool. Masterful leaders are great connectors. They are also great presenters, and they know how and when to show a touch of humanity. Masterful leaders trust, and are trusted in return.

Chapter 1: Listening

"We have two ears and one mouth, and we should use them in that proportion."
First Century Roman Philosopher Epictetus

Leaders need to listen in order to make effective and timely decisions. Some leaders, however, are better talkers than listeners. Every moment spent speaking is a moment forever lost to listening. Masterful leaders focus on learning and using effective listening skills. "Talk less and listen more" is sound advice for aspiring leaders.

1. **Listen at least 60% of the time.**

2. **Never interrupt a speaker.**

3. **Create a culture where staff speak their minds.**

Creating a good environment for listening is a start. In one-on-one meetings, make eye contact, ask leading questions, and focus on truly listening to the answers. Avoid impatience, checking the time, and cutting off the speaker in mid-sentence if you want to truly listen. Being really present and listening is hard work and takes practice. Many leaders don't bother.

In group meetings, create a safe environment for listening. Critiquing the speaker, cutting off statements or answers, and sarcasm are guaranteed to diminish opportunities for effective listening. These diminished opportunities often lead to poor, regrettable decisions.

Positive reinforcement, patience with the speaker, and questions intended to elicit the speaker's opinions are effective strategies for promoting a positive environment in which listening can flourish. When effective listening is present, better decisions follow. Effective listening is a learned skill. It is the ultimate show of respect. It is a foundation skill for masterful leadership.

Masterful leaders learn to listen carefully to patients, staff, and physicians. They connect daily whenever possible. They get out of their offices and into inpatient rooms and outpatient departments. They meet with staff, and they listen to physicians' concerns and ideas. They understand the enormous power of listening and acting upon what is learned. In a word, they connect.

The Power of Listening

A new CEO faced an urgent survival challenge shortly after he arrived to assume the leadership of the smaller hospital in a two-hospital community. A world-renowned health system purchased the larger hospital in town and community leaders openly questioned the need for both hospitals.

Instead of engaging in desperate tactics, the new CEO decided his hospital could thrive by becoming profoundly good at listening. He led a comprehensive listening initiative that engaged patients, staff, physicians, and members of the community. He listened carefully to critical feedback and suggestions. He catalogued strengths and weaknesses of his hospital and the competitor across town. From this listening experience, he crafted a simple competitive strategy of transforming his hospital into a world-class customer service enterprise. He asserted that "we should not compete, we should be better."

During the next decade, the smaller hospital got bigger. In five years, it equaled its competitor in market share. In five more years, it surpassed the competing hospital. During this transformational decade, the listening hospital earned national patient satisfaction and employee morale awards while achieving 10% operating margins. This success story is a stunning example of how listening led to transforming not just a hospital, but the healthcare delivery options for the community.

Chapter 2: Connecting with Patients

A much-neglected listening opportunity in healthcare organizations is listening to patients, our customers. Unfortunately, many leaders, especially senior executives, never even see, much less interact, with patients. In no other industry do leaders go to such great lengths to avoid customers. Masterful healthcare leaders always find ways to stay connected by listening to patients.

1. **See at least a few patients every week.**

2. **Listen to patients' concerns. Do something about them.**

3. **Expect direct reports to see patients every week, too.**

As leaders move up in title and responsibility, connecting with patients becomes more and more challenging. A good nursing unit director sees every patient, every day. A vice president of nursing has to work harder to devote a portion of the day to seeing and interacting with patients. A chief operating officer with multiple vice presidents reporting to him must work even harder at patient connectivity. For a chief executive officer, it is a monumental challenge to remain connected to patients.

Find a way to maintain patient connectivity. Walk around the organization and make a real effort to speak with inpatients and outpatients. Conduct regular focus groups of randomly selected patients. Make personal phone calls to recently treated patients to elicit opinions on their care. Make time to really listen to patients and respond to their positive and negative feedback. Masterful leaders always expect their direct reports to connect with patients too. In this manner, connectivity becomes part of the organization's culture.

Masterful physician leaders make time for patients too. Try hard to maintain some level of clinical practice or patient contact, avoiding, if possible, becoming a full-time executive. Find time to stay rooted in your medical profession by seeing clinical patients and by listening to their concerns and suggestions, even after attaining high executive office.

Masterful leaders are never too busy or too isolated to see patients and learn from them. Whether their job is to lead a department or a healthcare system, they appreciate that patients are the true reason their healthcare enterprise exists. Patients are our customers. Masterful leaders never lose that simple insight.

Priceless Hot Line

When I was a brand new, first-time hospital CEO, I had a special phone line installed in my office, just for patients. When inpatients were admitted, they received this number. My "hot line" was prominently displayed in the Emergency Room and outpatient waiting areas. This phone number was greatly appreciated by patients. They never abused it. Patients called either when they were especially pleased with their care or when they were really upset about something. Positive calls outnumbered negative calls five to one. I learned something from every call. Good calls provided an opportunity to thank specific staff members for their excellent work with patients. Negative calls provided an immediate opportunity to fix a problem. The hot line was in use during my entire five-year tenure. The listening opportunities it provided were priceless.

Chapter 3: Connecting with Staff

Masterful leaders are personally connected with staff and physicians. For front line supervisors, connecting is part of their daily routine to interact with staff and physicians. As leaders move up the organizational ladder, more effort must be invested to maintain personal connections with staff and physicians. The best leaders always find a way.

1. **Visit with staff at least once a week.**

2. **Leave your door open to drop-in visits.**

3. **Expect direct reports to visit personally with staff, too.**

Make it a priority to connect personally with staff. Don't delegate this connection. Find time to listen to and learn from staff. Some leaders connect by systematically walking around their organizations and stopping frequently to ask questions of staff and listening to concerns. Others ensure connection by holding regular "town hall" meetings with staff and physicians to both communicate and to listen. Still others make sure their office door is always open, literally and figuratively, to staff and physicians.

Make it a point to periodically and regularly visit staff and physicians around the clock and on weekends and holidays. Make off-hours staff feel appreciated by your presence, by positive reinforcement, and by listening to concerns and ideas. Masterful leaders expect their direct-report subordinates to do likewise.

It is all too easy for leaders to become isolated as they climb the organization ladder. For vice presidents with multiple departments, it is a challenge to regularly see the staff; for chief operating and chief executive officers, even more so. Masterful leaders never lose the desire to remain connected as they progress upward. They never allow themselves to be isolated. They understand that if staff are unable to bring concerns or suggestions to leaders, they lose confidence or they stop caring.

Masterful leaders learn and respond to feedback they receive from connecting with staff and physicians. Researchers Salovey and Mayer labeled this "emotional intelligence," and many authors, like Peter Druker, popularized the phrase. Masterful leaders turn emotional intelligence into action. Far from a negative, connectivity keeps masterful leaders in touch with the staff and physicians who care for patients. Listening to them is a tangible sign of respect.

Wall of Fame

A small hospital CEO had two great ideas for staying connected. On one office wall were photographs of every employee, taken on their first day on the job. There were over 300 photos, and the CEO worked hard to connect names and faces for each employee. He also conducted birthday lunches on Mondays for every employee who had a birthday that week. He loved those lunches and so did his employees. Every employee in that hospital felt a personal connection to their CEO, and much mutual learning took place at those lunches. In today's electronic world, perhaps a hospital website with all employees' photos would help leaders at all levels stay similarly connected to staff.

Chapter 4: Meetings

Masterful leaders run effective meetings. What are effective meetings? They start and finish on time, and they accomplish something of value. Absent these basics, meetings are a waste of valuable time.

1. **Start and end on time.**

2. **Restrict attendance to only those who matter to the discussion.**

3. **Arrange agendas in priority order and distribute in advance.**

Start on time. Masterful leaders insist on timeliness. To do otherwise penalizes those people who are on time. All meetings should have start and stop times. Meetings over 60 minutes, unless for an extraordinary purpose, often lose focus and effectiveness and should be avoided.

Everyone who attends a meeting should have a purpose. For most routine meetings, note takers are a waste of resources. Meetings should have an outcome: a decision, a consensus, a commitment, or a call to action. Most meetings have too many people, last too long, and accomplish nothing. Avoid "waste of time" meetings.

Meeting manners are important too. Taking calls, texting, tweeting, or answering e-mails during meetings are confirmation that meeting participants are not focusing on the meeting and should be excused. Sidebar conversations, the epitome of bad meeting manners, are never tolerated by masterful leaders.

Use agendas for all but the simplest and quickest meetings. Agendas should always be arranged in priority order, with the most important items first. This is especially critical for recurring meetings such as board meetings. It is easy to fall into the trap of using a meeting template that places "new business" at the end of the agenda. This is precisely the worst agenda placement for discussion of important new issues. The end of the meeting is when participants are most impatient and anxious to leave. Masterful leaders always ensure that the most important items are discussed first, when attention is most focused.

Regularly ask meeting participants for input on agendas and for post-meeting feedback. Encouraging honesty contributes to fine-tuning meeting agendas, formats, and purpose. Listen carefully to constructive feedback and make changes accordingly.

New Leaders; Better Meetings

A new board chairman and new CEO took office simultaneously. Both wanted to update the monthly board meeting format. For over a decade, board agendas followed the same template. Finance committee business dominated this board's meeting format. New business and the president's report, undeniably the most important parts of the meeting, were always at the very end. The new leaders changed the agenda format to:

- *Call to order*
- *Consent agenda*
- *President's report*
- *New business and discussion*
- *Medical staff report*
- *Committee reports*
- *Old business*
- *Adjournment*

Several very important improvements occurred with this new format. A consent agenda was added, allowing routine reports to be dispensed with quickly. The president's report was moved to the beginning of the meeting, followed by discussion time to be sure new business and priority items had ample time for quality discussion. After several months, board members agreed that meetings were more productive and interesting. They especially liked the discussion time portion of the agenda, which gave board members the opportunity to actively have a dialogue about issues, instead of merely hearing reports and voting "yes" on management's recommendations.

Chapter 5: Presentations

Leaders spend a good deal of their professional lives making presentations. Masterful leaders view every presentation as a four-point opportunity: #1. Present; #2. Discuss; #3. Listen; #4. Ask.

Many leaders never get beyond point number one. Enlightened leaders view presentations as learning opportunities, not just teaching opportunities. Regardless of whether the leader is a department director addressing employees in a monthly meeting or a CEO addressing the board of directors, presentations are precious opportunities not to be minimized.

1. **Practice out loud.**

2. **Make frequent eye contact.**

3. **Keep it short. Take and answer questions.**

First, decide on the appropriate presentation format. Some presentations are best handled with simple notes. Others may require a discussion outline. Still others may require PowerPoint slides. Use minimal words on the PowerPoint slide and never read the slide to your audience. Regardless of the format, there are several important points that distinguish presentations by masterful leaders from everyone else.

Practice the presentation. Don't just lip read either; practice the presentation out loud and often enough to be comfortable with the material. Deliver the presentation at eye level whenever possible. In all but the largest gatherings, that means sitting down instead of standing. Eye level presentations are more conversational for the audience. When making a PowerPoint presentation, avoid using handouts. Your audience will focus more on the handouts than you. Make handouts available after you finish.

Make frequent eye contact during presentations. Engage your audience. Make everyone in the audience feel like they are the focus of the presentation. Keep it short and interesting. Use presentations as an opportunity to discuss and listen to feedback. Presenting masterful leaders actively engage in learning, not just speaking. Always ask for feedback. Encourage questions and never duck the hard questions. Understand that the Q&A at the end of every effective presentation is the most valuable time of the presentation, for both presenter and audience.

Exceptionally Crafted Request

A department director for cardiovascular services was especially adept at making presentations. A board presentation to request approval for a third cardiac catheterization lab was an excellent example of effective presentations. The director began with a brief overview of the hospital's cardiac program, with specific emphasis on catheterizations. The presentation progressed to historical and future catheterization volume projections. Financial implications were presented next. Two key physicians joined the presentation to articulate the clinical implications of a third cath lab. Next, a Q&A segment followed to actively solicit board member questions. The Q&A became the highlight of the presentation. The requested cath lab approval was granted. Not only did board members approve, they learned valuable insights about their hospital's cardiac programs.

Chapter 6: Continuous Updating

How is it possible to update employees and physicians if they number in the hundreds? Even thousands? The answer? By using a combination of approaches from personal to electronic, and by continuously connecting. The biggest continuous updating challenge lies with the organization's CEO.

1. **Hold town hall meetings regularly.**

2. **Be open to any and all questions. Use answers to educate.**

3. **Use e-mail and podcasts.**

Personal communication is always best. "Town hall" style meetings work well, even if the organization employs thousands. Town hall meetings are a big commitment for CEOs. Masterful leaders do them three or four times a year. Having a prepared presentation on the status of the organization, current challenges, and future plans is a great agenda format. Beyond prepared remarks, these meetings are a wonderful question-and-answer opportunity. Taking questions from the staff provides an opportunity to allay rumors and stimulate positive thinking. Culture and values are reinforced during these meetings. For employees unable to attend, a video should be provided, accessible on the organization's website so that every employee can feel connected.

Dropping in on regularly scheduled department or division meetings is another great opportunity for updating staff. Most or all departments have regularly scheduled meetings. Take advantage of these meetings to make drop-in appearances. Even in large organizations, drop-in appearances by vice presidents or senior leadership can contribute to keeping the staff updated.

Weekly or monthly e-mail newsletters can be used to update employees and physicians on matters of interest and importance. A "message from the CEO" column can be very effective in highlighting areas of major importance. Care should be taken to ensure that all members of the staff have e-mail access. The organization must have and update current e-mail addresses for all staff. For those few employees who do not have access to a personal e-mail account, organization-access computers should be provided. Video "podcast" updates can also be effectively used to update the staff.

Walking around is a superb way for leaders to personally engage in continuously updating staff. Spending a few hours a week visiting staff, on different shifts and in different locations throughout the organization, gives masterful leaders a personal opportunity to listen to concerns and deliver impromptu updates.

Exceptional Updating

A CEO devoted 10% of his time to continuously updating staff, physicians, and the community. He wrote a weekly e-mail newsletter for routine updates. He attended three departmental meetings a month to stay connected and, over the course of a year, he made sure he attended at least one meeting for every department. He conducted town hall meetings for physicians and staff quarterly. He relished the Q&A portion of these meetings and never ducked tough questions. Every six months he conducted updates for business, political, and religious leaders of the community. And at least once a year he held town hall meetings for the community, inviting all interested residents to hear future plans for their community hospital. Continuous updating was and is a priority for this CEO. He is very much appreciated for his openness and transparency.

Chapter 7: A Touch of Humanity

Leaders all have the opportunity to show humanity. Some take this opportunity and some do not. A leader can be obsessed with results, extraordinary financial performance, great quality and service metrics, and still regularly show a touch of humanity.

1. **Write personal notes often.**

2. **Spend some unscripted time with direct reports.**

3. **Thank staff for a job well done.**

E-mail has become the communication vehicle of choice for most leaders, most of the time. To show a touch of humanity, try using hand-written notes. Everyone has a birthday: a good reason to send a hand-written note. Remember those close to you in the organization with a personal birthday note or card. Writing a sentence or two only takes a minute, yet a personal note can have a profoundly positive impact.

Use the phone more often than the "reply" button on the e-mail window. If something is important, call and have a discussion. Better yet, if the issue is really important, personally visit the other person. Many people, sitting in the same office location, communicate by e-mail instead of face-to-face. Even people literally next door to each other communicate with e-mail. How tragic. E-mail is fine for small issues. Phone or face-to-face contact is better for important issues.

The gift of time is another touch of humanity opportunity. Masterful leaders spend personal time with colleagues and subordinates. No agenda necessary--just sit and have an open-ended discussion. Get to know your direct reports. Let them get to know you. Inquire about family, and life outside work. This time will be remembered and appreciated. Go visit people in their offices or workspaces. A spontaneous visit with no agenda is a personal touch of humanity. Use it frequently.

There are some events in a person's life that deserve more than e-mail. If a subordinate or colleague loses a family member, take a few moments to send a real sympathy card, with a real hand-written note of comfort. If practical, show up at the wake or funeral. Use your personal presence as a touch of humanity.

Perhaps the greatest opportunity to show humanity is to recognize a job well done. A personal call, note, or small gift: all can be used to show appreciation to a colleague or subordinate. Masterful leaders understand these small touches of humanity will be remembered, and repaid.

Setting the Example

A new CEO of a large tertiary hospital with 6,000 employees looked for a symbol to demonstrate a touch of humanity. The leadership was under extreme stress because the hospital was failing. When he took office, he had a list created for birthdays of board members, administration, department directors, and physician chairs. The list had 250 names. The CEO sent a personal birthday greeting and three roses to everyone on that list, every year. It was a small touch of humanity, an opportunity to say "thank you" for their fine work and dedication. He received many "thank yous" in return, many on hand-written note cards.

Chapter 8: Confidentiality and Trust

Confidentiality is a little like hand-written notes today--rarely used in leadership. Masterful leaders understand the value of confidentiality. It is a tool to achieve better organization results through creating an environment of trust.

1. **Never betray a confidence.**

2. **Create a culture where staff confide when concerned.**

3. **Have a close circle for absolutely confidential discussions.**

Confidentiality is a hard concept to grasp today. E-mail, Facebook, YouTube, Google, and the endless variety of electronic communication portals make confidentiality extraordinarily challenging. At the push of a key, the most confidential communications can be broadcast to the world, sometimes with disastrous consequences.

Masterful leaders understand that confidentiality begins with one person sharing information with another. Confidential information is intelligence that can be used to modify existing decisions or to make better decisions. However, the source of confidential information must always be protected. If it isn't, useful confidential information may evaporate.

All leaders need a circle of subordinates with whom they can have confidential discussions and debates about critical matters. The debate may be about strategy. It may be about finances. It may be about staff or physicians. This circle of confidentiality must be absolute. There must be a bond of trust that is never broken within the confidentiality circle.

Confidentiality in healthcare organizations is extraordinarily important. Masterful healthcare leaders create a culture in which confidentiality of patient information is sacred and never violated. Patient confidentiality must be understood and protected by every member of the organization, from staff to physicians and even volunteers and vendors.

Trust, in an organization, is the ability to communicate information without fear. Fear of retribution, fear of confidentiality breach, or fear of compromising the organization. Confidentiality is based on trust, and trust is a cultural value that is never compromised by masterful leaders. An environment of trust and confidentiality is absolutely essential because it allows information that could be potentially explosive to flow to the right decision makers. Sometimes, that can be the difference between life and death for patients.

Unforeseen Consequences

A newly promoted chief nursing officer was visited shortly after taking office by an operating room nurse. The nurse shared, in confidence, his concerns about an aging heart surgeon. He said that he had reported his concerns in confidence to the CNO's predecessor. Shortly after that first discussion, the surgeon threatened to have the nurse fired. The nurse's confidence had obviously been broken by the former CNO, but he decided to try again with the new CNO. The second confidential discussion led to an appropriate investigation. The outcome was that the surgeon was judged to be no longer able to safely practice. Unfortunately, the investigation also determined harm had been done to several patients between the first and second "confidential" reports.

PRACTICING LEADERSHIP

Leadership is action and effect. It is not a state of mind. Leadership is a dynamic movement of people and things, to accomplish desired outcomes. Practicing leadership is a series of actions, beginning with the acquisition of working knowledge. Masterful leaders are able to simplify and grasp the essence of getting things done through others. They begin by acquiring working knowledge, followed by setting expectations and demanding accountability. A keen sense of situational awareness is a prerequisite for making good decisions. Planning effectively for the future is also an essential skill for masterful leadership. Masterful leaders integrate all of these critical skills to accomplish desired outcomes for their organizations.

Chapter 9: Working Knowledge

Masterful leaders have a well-grounded knowledge of the processes, people, and outcomes for all areas under their responsibility. Starting at the department director level, leaders should understand the service provided, the processes needed to deliver the service, the people who deliver the service, and the desired outcomes for the service.

1. **Know and respect the staff in all areas of your responsibility.**

2. **Spend quality time learning new areas of responsibility.**

3. **Listen to staff. They will teach you well.**

For an imaging department, the director must have a sound working knowledge of all modalities from chest X-rays to MRIs and everything in between. The director must understand the department's processes from patient scheduling to clinical results reporting to quality assurance and all the steps to achieve desired results for patients. The director also should possess a working knowledge of the history of the department and how it has evolved to its present state. If the director was recruited from the outside, he should take the time to learn the department's history as part of a thorough orientation.

At the vice president level, leaders should take the time to become very familiar with every department under their responsibility. This takes much more effort than a few visits and superficial meetings. It takes quality time immersed in each department to learn about its services, processes, people, and outcomes. Every new vice president is wise to make this investment in time at the beginning of his tenure and every time a new department is added to his responsibilities.

Working knowledge becomes an especially great challenge for chief operating and chief executive officers. Nonetheless, it is critical for them to possess working knowledge of all areas they oversee. Working knowledge allows them to ask the right questions at the right time to ensure the areas under their responsibility are functioning at their optimum levels of quality and service to patients.

Masterful leaders take great effort to keep working knowledge current. They walk the halls and visit departments, talking to staff, physicians, and with patients and patients' families. They constantly seek real time information about how their enterprise is fulfilling its mission. They listen and act upon what they learn.

Humble Career Start

As a newly graduated MBA, I reported for duty to the hospital's CEO. Instead of being assigned a nice office and a secretary, I was issued a pair of heavy-duty rubber gloves and told to report to the food service director for patient tray breakdown duty. It occurred to me that I had reported for duty in "The Twilight Zone." For the next two weeks, as I wondered where my career was headed, I emptied patient meal trays, loaded the dishwasher, and took out the trash. The CEO summoned me to his office at the beginning of week three to ask what I had learned. "I learned what patients don't like to eat," I replied. "Not bad," the CEO said. "Perhaps there is hope for you." For the next five years, I spent many hours, days, and weeks learning new departments. I polished floors with the housekeeping staff, learned to draw blood with the laboratory phlebotomists, helped the night shift nursing supervisor find beds for emergency admissions, and followed up delinquent patient accounts with the business office manager. Six years after breaking down patient meal trays, I found myself in the chief operating officer position at age 29, with a working knowledge of every department of the hospital.

Chapter 10: Setting Expectations

Leaders must set high expectations--for themselves, direct reports, and the entire organization. Expectations come in two forms: cultural and performance. Cultural expectations are the foundation of the organization's value system. Leaders must hold direct reports accountable for living within the organization's value system and for being living examples of the organization's culture. Performance expectations are assigned priorities from the leader to his direct reports. Masterful leaders attend to both kinds of expectations.

1. **Articulate expectations.**

2. **Be sure they are understood and "owned."**

3. **Give equal weight to cultural and performance expectations.**

Set high performance expectations that are challenging to achieve. Articulate timelines to monitor progress for achieving expectations. Seek input from your direct reports when setting expectations. This creates ownership, making the expectations mutual instead of top-down edicts.

Collectively, a masterful leader's performance expectations for all direct reports form the basis for achieving organizational success. Overall success depends on each direct report doing his job to achieve individual expectations. Setting expectations cannot be delegated. Articulate performance expectations that, when achieved, ensure the success of the individual and the organization.

For an emergency department director, performance expectations may be set for patient throughput times, efficient test utilization, and percentage of patients who leave without being seen. These expectations become the basis for judging the quality and service of the department and staff. For a vice president of nursing, performance expectations may be set for patient quality outcomes and staff turnover. For a chief executive, performance expectations may be expressed in terms of market share, financial performance, and clinical quality indicators.

Stress the importance of cultural expectations, too. If direct reports do not meet cultural expectations, the organization's value system is compromised. When values are compromised, the culture itself is compromised. Cultural expectations may be expressed in terms of staff and physician morale and patient satisfaction scores. Masterful leaders ensure that cultural expectations receive the same attention and commitment as performance expectations. Fulfilling both types of expectations ensures the success of the organization.

New Sheriff in Town

A new vice president began working with his direct report department managers shortly after his arrival. One of his first priorities was to review annual employee performance evaluations completed by his managers. In one department, he observed that virtually all of the employees were rated "5" on a scale of 1 – 5. When the vice president challenged the department manager's evaluations, he was met with silence. The vice president set the new expectation that he wanted honest and truthful evaluations for all employees. He wondered out loud whether it was possible for everyone to be perfect. The department manager did all the evaluations over with honesty as the principal guideline. Upon reviewing the new evaluations, the vice president noted that there were some star performers, a number of average performers, and a few employees who needed to improve or depart. He then proceeded to give the manager his first truly honest performance review of his career. The manager responded extremely well and focused on reinforcing his strengths and improving his leadership weaknesses. The following year, to no one's surprise, the department staff's performance reviews were honest and the overall performance of the department was much improved.

Chapter 11: Accountability

Accountability is one of the most important tools for masterful leaders. Leaders who hold themselves and their direct reports truly accountable are rare. It takes great discipline and commitment to be personally accountable and to demand accountability in others. Masterful leaders have ample measures of both.

1. **Set defined goals.**

2. **Measure performance.**

3. **Reward accomplishment. Ensure failure has consequences.**

The first step in achieving accountability is to identify parameters for which accountability is to be applied. For a business office director, it may be a financial parameter such as days in accounts receivable. For an emergency department director, it may be a customer service parameter such as percentile ranking of customer service quality. For an operating room manager, it may be a clinical quality parameter such as the rate of hospital-acquired infections following surgery. Accountability begins when a leader and direct report agree on the parameters, measurement methodology, and the desired results.

The next step in the accountability process is measurement of performance vs. the desired result. Masterful leaders regularly discuss progress and results with direct reports. They instill a sense of responsibility for achieving desired results within expected timelines. When final results are in, either desired outcomes are achieved or they are not. If they are achieved, positive feedback is forthcoming and a decision is made to either maintain current results or raise the bar to a new and higher level of performance.

If desired results are not achieved, there should be analysis to determine why. Potentially, there should be consequences. Masterful leaders apply excellent judgment in these circumstances. The direct report may be given more time and more assistance. Or, it may be decided that the direct report has failed. Depending on the seriousness of the failure, the direct report may be disciplined or removed from his position.

Knowing when to give more time and more resources or to declare failure and move on is a judgment that masterful leaders make without hesitation. Lesser leaders rarely declare failure. They make excuses, lower expectations, or blame themselves when a direct report fails to be accountable.

Ticking Time Bomb

An emergency medicine medical director made a decision by not acting. A physician under his direction had poorly controlled diabetes. This physician's blood sugar levels regularly got so low they affected the physician's ability to function and to communicate coherently. Instead of acting decisively to address the problem the director ignored it. He depended on staff working with the physician to monitor his behavior. Nurses were instructed to tell the physician to check his blood sugar levels and eat something if he began acting strangely. Watching out for this impaired physician even became part of the orientation for new nurses. The department director knew of the problem. So did the chief nursing officer. So did the chief medical officer. No one acted to intervene for more than a year. A time bomb waiting to blow up--all because no one accepted accountability to deal with this impaired physician.

Chapter 12: Consistency Is Good, Complacency Is Bad

Masterful leaders are consistent. Having strong values, living by those values, and consistently applying values over time enables the organization's staff to fulfill its mission. The absence of either values or their consistent application can result in confusion and frustration.

1. **Be consistent enough that your staff knows what is expected.**

2. **Never allow complacency to dull passion for success.**

3. **If you become complacent, get over it fast or go away.**

Masterful leaders can be authoritarian or participative, or somewhere in between, as long as they are consistent. A hard driving authoritarian can be effective if he selects direct reports who flourish under this style of leadership. Likewise, a more participative leader can flourish too, as long as he selects the right direct reports. But try mixing authoritarian and participative leadership styles and confusion becomes rampant. Staff members are unable to function and chaos follows.

Departing from consistency always results in diminished organizational performance. In the worst case scenario, the staff has no clue what the leader wants and may stop functioning. In successful organizations, staff always know what their leader expects and try to fulfill these expectations. Consistency is good. It facilitates fulfilling of expectations and achieving an organization's goals.

Complacency, on the other hand, is the enemy of successful leaders. When an organization is meeting its goals, the risk of complacency is greatest. Complacent leaders take success for granted. They believe they have all the answers. They believe they are infallible. They are wrong.

Never succumb to complacency. Always strive to do better and to elicit better performance from direct reports. Staff members sense complacency and emulate it. Quality suffers, service suffers, morale suffers, and performance atrophies. Reset goals when they are achieved. Never be completely satisfied. Never rest upon laurels. Masterful leaders know complacency is bad, for themselves and for their organizations.

From Complacency to Near Ruin

In a two-hospital market, both hospitals had 50% market share for two decades. Then one of the hospitals hired a new CEO, who began using aggressive marketing and physician alignment strategies. Over time these strategies worked very well. The second hospital was complacent. Its leaders believed it would always be able to sustain its 50% market share. They were wrong. When their market share declined to 40%, the hospital's sponsoring system replaced the CEO. When it declined to 30%, another new CEO was hired. When it declined to 20%, the system replaced the CEO for the third time in five years. The failing hospital's staff and physicians became completely discouraged with the rapidly revolving door in the administrative suite. When market share reached a low of 15%, a full-scale turnaround was launched with yet another new CEO. The turnaround barely succeeded in saving the 115-year-old complacent hospital from bankruptcy and closure.

Chapter 13: Effective Subordinate Skills

All leaders report to someone. CEOs report to boards. Department directors report to vice presidents. Vice presidents report to chief operating officers, and so on. Masterful leaders function as great subordinates, as well as great leaders.

1. **Finish assignments early.**

2. **Anticipate your superior's needs.**

3. **Always tell the truth.**

Set aside time and energy for subordinate duties. Listen to your superior's feedback and aspirations for the future. Seek advice and counsel from your superior, especially in situations where he holds teaching and mentoring as part of his value system.

Several attributes are always appreciated by one's superior. Complete assignments early. No one ever gets in trouble for finishing an assignment before it is due. Always be dependable in execution. If you are asked to do something, do it immediately and make sure the desired outcome is achieved. Never place a superior in a position of being surprised by bad news. Meeting regularly, supplemented by frequent phone and e-mail contact, should avoid this eventuality. Anticipate the future needs of your superior. Don't wait for instructions when it is clear your superior will benefit from a piece of information, an action, or from you taking an initiative.

The most valued attribute in a subordinate is always telling the truth. In theory, this should be easy. In practice, it can be extraordinarily challenging. Why? Telling the truth often means delivering bad news. Masterful leaders cultivate truth-telling in their subordinates. They want bad news and never punish subordinates for delivering it. Telling the truth takes courage, especially when the truth involves unwelcome news. Subordinates must always find the courage to tell the truth. These subordinates become masterful leaders.

Genuinely seeking to assist one's superior to succeed in his role, and doing everything possible as a subordinate to support that outcome, is a hallmark of an exceptional subordinate...and a future masterful leader. No matter how high the executive leader rises, including to the position of CEO, attention to subordinate skills is important and always appreciated.

Well Placed Honesty

A system CEO joined a leadership team that had several seasoned veterans and several new division presidents. The newest division president on the team had tremendous people skills, and his staff of vice presidents and directors was dedicated to both his and the organization's success. The new system CEO quickly learned that the young president was honest and fearless when providing critical feedback. On many occasions during his first year in office, the president provided invaluable critical feedback to the CEO. The critical feedback was always well articulated and delivered in private. The CEO came to admire and respect this young president's ability to constructively criticize and deliver honest feedback without being offensive. The CEO benefited from this subordinate's honesty, and the organization's progress during his first critical year was greatly enhanced by the president's candid feedback.

Chapter 14: Situational Awareness

Why are leaders surprised when they are fired? They lack situational awareness. They missed the clues. They did not see termination coming; otherwise they would surely have acted differently. Lack of situational awareness is a serious shortcoming in life, both personal and professional.

1. **Listen very carefully to staff.**

2. **Integrate informal feedback with formal communication channels.**

3. **Be sure bad news percolates to you.**

In aviation, perfectly good airplanes are crashed and lives are lost because pilots lost situational awareness. Careers also have ended prematurely from a similar loss of professional situational awareness.

Masterful leaders know their strengths and weaknesses. They constantly gather and process "emotional intelligence," giving them a clear picture of where they and their organization stand at all times. This situational awareness picture enables leaders to make excellent decisions and to lead effectively. Loss of situational awareness always leads to bad results. Sometimes the loss can lead to poor decisions. At other times, loss of situational awareness can be fatal.

Work hard to never lose sight of your organization's situational picture. Do not allow yourself to become isolated. Cultivate diverse sources of information, both through formal channels and through informal observations. For example, if a leader wishes to understand if any staff are cheating on payroll practices, he should ask the payroll clerks who process paychecks. If he wants to know if there are any impaired surgeons escaping notice, asking the scrub nurses actively doing surgery cases is a logical step. If he wants a reading on the culture when leaders are mostly absent, he should ask the night shift nursing supervisor. Informal feedback, when added to formal communications and reports, paints a much more complete situational picture than formal feedback alone.

Constantly connect with members of the leadership team, physicians, staff, and patients. Process feedback and update your situational awareness picture with every interaction. Seek bad news, as well as good news. Never allow small problems to grow into big, insurmountable problems. Make decisions based on the most current and complete information available. Masterful leaders take great care to maintain the most accurate and complete situational awareness picture.

Beauty Parlor Fiasco

A CEO probably broke a record for short tenure by getting fired 60 days after starting his new job. He distinguished himself by not fitting in from day one. He wore pinstriped suits to work; his board members and physicians wore string ties and cowboy boots. He was patrician in manner; his staff were rugged individualists who valued "roll up the sleeves" leaders. The CEO talked down to everyone he met, from physicians to community leaders to employees and volunteers. His situational awareness shortcomings were surpassed only by his wife's. At the local beauty parlor, the nexus of community spirit, she declared during her first hair appointment that she was making a very big sacrifice to live in "this hick town." Board members, whose wives frequented the beauty parlor, quickly relieved her misery by convening a special board meeting to fire the new CEO. The only person surprised by his termination was the clueless CEO.

Chapter 15: Making Decisions

Leaders understand the importance of making timely decisions. They must not delay, obsess about data, or try to avoid the risk of making decisions. Masterful leaders know the value of when to say "yes" and when to say "no," and to do so promptly.

1. **Don't delay decisions.**

2. **Learn to make decisions like physicians.**

3. **Don't worry about what other people think. Worry about what you think.**

Most decisions in healthcare enterprises can be made in a few hours, or at most, a few days. Emulate physicians when it comes to decision-making. Many life or death decisions are made by physicians in minutes or hours. Especially complicated clinical decisions may take a few days. Emergency room physicians and trauma surgeons are especially skilled decision makers under pressure.

Some healthcare leaders allow even simple decisions to take weeks, months, or even years, especially when endless meetings are convened and committees are formed. Do not delay decisions. Gather data, listen to opinions, and study the facts. Evaluate implications. Then make the decision. Don't be afraid of making a wrong decision.

Masterful leaders value good counsel when making decisions. For profoundly important decisions, listen to your trusted advisors. Listen to direct reports' informed points of view. Listen to your own counsel. Some leaders trust their "guts" when making decisions. Some guts admittedly are better than others. Pay attention to your gut when making important decisions.

Masterful leaders make 80% or more of their decisions correctly. The remaining 20% are fixed after the fact as necessary. Leaders should learn from their mistaken decisions and move forward. Trust direct reports to make decisions and stand behind those decisions without second-guessing.

Not making a decision is really a decision in itself. The absence of a decision can be catastrophic. A delayed decision in the emergency room can result in the death of a patient. A delayed strategic decision in the boardroom can cause the death of the enterprise. Masterful leaders never delay. They say "yes" or they say "no." They never say "maybe later" or hold on to a bad decision. And they never worry about who will get angry and who will criticize their decision after the fact.

Some leaders try to do the right thing. Other leaders do the nice thing. Masterful leaders always do the right thing, nicely.

From Worst of Times to Best of Times

A new CEO faced a profoundly important decision soon after taking office in his first CEO position. The hospital's emergency room physicians were provided by a large contract staffing company. The physicians were not residency-trained. They did not live in the community. They had uniformly poor attitudes. The emergency room nursing staff and hospital medical staff were extremely frustrated, but were convinced they could not find better emergency physicians. The new CEO made the decision to fire the contract group and was told by the group's president that he would never be able to recruit quality, residency-trained physicians to his small town. It took a year--a miserable year while problems went from bad to worse as the hospital searched for new emergency physicians. Finally, three graduating emergency medicine residents who wanted to stay together and form a new group were recruited. The new physicians arrived and succeeded, and the miserable recruiting year was quickly forgotten. Patients were the great beneficiaries of this decision.

Chapter 16: Planning

At every level within the organization, leaders should accept and embrace the responsibility for planning. A department director should be the chief planner for his department. A vice president should be the chief planner for his division. Planning the future is a critical skill for masterful leadership.

1. **Articulate a vision for the future.**

2. **Listen to internal wisdom before hiring consultants.**

3. **Execute plans with discipline.**

CEOs are the chief strategists for their organizations. This responsibility cannot be delegated to a vice president or a partner in a strategic planning consulting firm. While vice presidents and consultants can contribute positively, the CEO must envision the future of the organization and create the capability to achieve that future state.

Masterful leaders have a clear and firm grasp of where their organization must go to achieve and sustain success. This vision of the future state can be reduced to a few words or sentences and need not fill endless planning manuals and data tables. Articulate your vision's essence in clear and compelling words that inspire and motivate the organization to follow. This is as true for a single department as it is for the entire enterprise.

Articulating a vision is the first step in planning, but only the first step. Leaders must ensure that they have the resources to achieve the vision. In some cases the resources are already available; in some other cases they must be brought into the organization. Once the resources are present, move relentlessly forward to achieve the future vision. Along this journey, identify steps and milestones to achieve the vision, and communicate progress throughout the organization so that everyone owns the vision and is part of creating the future.

Where do the steps and milestones come from to achieve a vision of the future? From wisdom that resides within the organization. Instead of hiring a planning consultant, mine the ideas of your staff, physicians, middle management, and administration. While consultants can be useful as facilitators and technical advisors, they rarely have the history and insights to plan the organization's future.

Internal stakeholders have the history, the insights, and, most importantly, the wisdom to create and implement a great plan for the future. Recognize this and give them the opportunity to contribute. Masterful leaders appreciate that if internal stakeholders help build the plan, they will execute it with vigor and enthusiasm.

Think Big; Act Big

In a three-hospital community, the market was dominated by the largest hospital, an investor-owned, for-profit facility. The two smaller hospitals were nonprofit, religiously sponsored facilities. The CEO of the smallest hospital conceived a big vision. He wanted to make his hospital the strongest financially and the hospital known for the highest quality patient care in the community. He embarked on a five-year plan to execute this vision, and he succeeded, with the full buy-in of his staff and medical staff. He then designed a merger strategy with the other larger, nonprofit hospital. His hospital was the surviving entity, and he became its CEO. When the merger was completed, the combined new hospital was larger and had stronger financial and clinical performance than the once dominant for-profit hospital. This market was profoundly changed, due to the planning and flawless execution of one visionary leader.

PEOPLE LEADERSHIP

Organization charts, information systems, strategic plans, and consulting reports don't take care of patients. People do. Staff and physicians deliver care. Countless support staff also play an important role in delivering patient care. The leader's job is to hire the best people, teach them well, give them clear goals, and evaluate how well they do. Masterful leaders obsess about people. They set an exceptional personal example, and they don't hesitate to fire people who don't perform, while recognizing that firing is a failure of leadership. The best leaders get trusted advice when they need it and they listen with great attention to the wisdom of their own staff, physicians, and customers.

Chapter 17: Hiring

Hiring direct report subordinates is one of a leader's most important duties. Never delegate this priority to human resource departments or executive search consultants. Become intimately involved in the hiring process. Seek direct reports who have the potential to replace you someday, the best and the brightest candidates you can find. Masterful leaders look for intelligence, judgment, loyalty, high energy and the ability not to just solve problems, but to anticipate them.

1. **Hire the best people.**

2. **Make personal reference checks and visits.**

3. **Trust your gut.**

Personal interviews are the cornerstone of successful hiring. Prepare by reviewing background information and resumes and performing Internet background searches. Prepare interview questions in advance and know what you are looking for in responses. Probe the candidate's history, and don't be afraid to pose provocative questions. Gauge chemistry during interviews and learn to "trust your gut" when it comes to evaluating the candidate's compatibility with yourself and the organization.

Thorough reference checking is a necessity. Call candidate references personally instead of delegating this critical task. References can and do lie. The only way to judge the veracity of the reference is to be on the line personally and listen very carefully.

A rarely exercised strategy when hiring is the personal visit. What better way is there for a vice president to judge a food service director candidate than to make a personal visit to the candidate's hospital to sample the food? If a CEO is hiring a chief nursing officer, how better to judge the candidate's values than to talk with their staff and judge the culture the candidate has created at his current hospital? Personal visits to a candidate's place of employment can be challenging to arrange, but masterful leaders find a way to observe firsthand the candidate's accomplishments. We can all be fooled by practiced interview skills and less than honest reference checks. It is much harder to be fooled during a personal visit.

Conduct at least two personal interviews before hiring. The second interview should always include the candidate's spouse or significant other/partner. The candidate's spouse is a window to the candidate's character. Always look through that window. Seek input from your other direct reports and from the staff who will be working for the prospective candidate. When all the input is in, masterful leaders are comfortable making the hiring decision.

Arrange for a thorough orientation after the offer is extended and accepted. Orientation is an integral part of a successful hire. Ensure that the new hire is properly welcomed and that the organization is well prepared for the newly hired person's arrival. A proper orientation sets the stage for future success.

Lesser of Two Evils?

A large medical center conducted a CEO search using a big name executive search firm. Multiple candidate panels were presented to the board search committee. Over a dozen candidates were interviewed. After searching for more than 12 months, two finalist candidates were presented to the board. The search firm did a less-than-stellar job in reference checking the two finalists, and the board made no personal reference calls. One candidate's hospital was discovered to have recent Medicare billing fraud problems. The other candidate was discovered to have had past womanizing problems and a legal problem, also related to billing fraud, in the distant past. These problems were never fully disclosed to the board search committee, who selected and hired one of the two finalists. Unfortunately, the candidate selected proved to have personal indiscretion problems that surfaced shortly after his hiring. His tenure was very short.

Chapter 18: Teaching and Mentoring

Leaders should be the teachers-in-chief for their areas of responsibility. Teaching values and skills enables leaders to disseminate and reinforce the organization's culture.

1. **Set a good example.**

2. **Regard teaching as a most important job.**

3. **Spend quality time planning your staff's development.**

Masterful leaders use teaching and mentoring as a communication strategy. Know what and when to teach. This is an art and requires forethought and investment of valuable leadership time. Each direct report should be taught and mentored as a strategy to enhance strengths and mitigate weaknesses. Above all, teach direct reports to be truthful and to speak up when any kind of problem or opportunity presents itself.

Masterful leaders spend quality time thinking about direction, assignments, and coaching for direct reports. Teaching and mentoring are effective long-term development strategies that benefit the entire organization, as well as the individual direct report. Always maintain and update a development plan for each direct report. This plan should include initiatives to develop strengths and diminish weaknesses.

The most precious teaching and mentoring strategy is spending quality one-on-one time. Including the direct report in meetings and situations that have learning value is also important. Bringing administrative interns, residents, or junior executives into the organization can be a very effective way to mentor future talent. Masterful leaders also fully appreciate the generational differences that exist and must be understood if teaching and learning are to be mutually effective. Teaching and mentoring are core values of every masterful leader. The higher the leader's position, the more challenging it is to find time for this. Mentoring and teaching take effort. The results are well worth this effort.

Sing Along CEO

A CEO was trying to set a very positive example for his vice presidents and department directors. He was especially concerned with teaching them connectivity with staff and patients. During the course of a year, he personally spent time in each department of his hospital, learning and observing. One of the departments was hospice. He spent the day with his hospice nursing staff monitoring and attending to dying patients at home. On one home visit, the CEO was called upon to pet the family dog while treatment was rendered. At another home, the CEO joined hands with the staff and family to sing a gospel hymn to a dying patient. He was fully present, setting a profoundly good mentoring example. His staff, management, and physicians told the hospice story for years afterward. It was a legendary teaching moment.

Chapter 19: Evaluating

Truly objective evaluations are among the most powerfully effective tools available to any leader. Unfortunately, they are rarely used to their full potential. An effective evaluation begins with the setting and mutual understanding of expectations. It ends with telling the truth.

1. **Set goals and expectations.**

2. **Provide truthful feedback.**

3. **Act on evaluation results.**

Effective evaluations combine both performance and cultural expectations. Both are critical. A direct report who meets all of his assigned performance goals but who is an ingrate as a person is not effective. A direct report who epitomizes the organization's culture but never meets targets is equally ineffective.

Ensure that your direct reports understand the organization's culture and values. This should be accomplished in the form of a good orientation and ongoing teaching and mentoring. Define goals and objectives for each direct report and timelines for accomplishing the objectives. Input on goals from direct reports is important. Goals should be mutually agreed upon and committed to writing.

Provide regular feedback to your direct reports. Monthly feedback is ideal. Quarterly feedback will suffice. Feedback should include a review of both cultural performance as well as performance vs. agreed-upon goals.

An annual review should include both an oral and written assessment of your direct report's performance. This is where average leaders fall short. They cannot bring themselves to be honest. They make excuses for poor performance or blame themselves. Masterful leaders are always truthful with direct reports, even if it hurts.

Objective evaluations either confirm good performance or confirm that performance has fallen short. Good performance should be appropriately rewarded and celebrated. Poor performance should be cause for evaluating whether the direct report is suitable for retention. Multiple poor evaluations are cause to fire the direct report. The secret of effective evaluation is telling the truth.

No Pain, No Gain

A few months after assuming office, a hospital president completed performance evaluations on his vice presidents. As was his custom, he articulated positive and negative attributes and identified areas for improvement. Upon receiving his performance review, one of the vice presidents was devastated. The president identified the vice president as a very positive force for change and that he conducted himself in a very positive and self-assured manner. On the negative side, the president pointed out that the vice president easily became frustrated and had trouble implementing some initiatives. Apparently, this was the first really candid evaluation the vice president had ever received. At first, the vice president was frustrated and defensive. Over the next several months, he was able to reflect on the negative feedback and implement changes to improve his effectiveness. By the following year, the vice president looked forward to receiving the constructive criticism and appreciated the effort made by the president to mentor and improve his performance. An intended consequence was that the vice president's evaluations of his department directors improved significantly, too.

Chapter 20: Firing

Firing represents failure. It may be a failure of hiring. It may be a failure of setting expectations or mentoring that did not take. It may be a failure of the evaluation process. But make no mistake: the necessity to fire someone is a failure of leadership. Firing is never easy. But there are times that firing a direct report is best for the organization. Weak leaders and weak organizations never seem to be able to make the firing decision. They avoid it by transferring the poor performer to a different position: out of sight, out of mind.

1. **Fire direct reports who don't perform or behave badly.**

2. **Treat fired persons with dignity.**

3. **Learn what went wrong and fix it.**

Masterful leaders are clear about expectations and truthful in their evaluations. If performance has not measured up, it is time for the direct report to go. Sometimes a subordinate sees clearly that he is not going to meet expectations and does the smart and honorable thing: he resigns. This is the exception, not the rule. Failing direct reports rarely have the situational awareness to know and admit to themselves they are failing. In these cases, the leader must fire the failing direct report.

There are certain unforgivable sins that masterful leaders never ignore. If a direct report lies, steals, or engages in bad behaviors inconsistent with the organization's culture, he should be fired with no second chances. If direct reports accept any of these bad behaviors in their subordinates, they should also be fired. Masterful leaders give no "second chances" for lack of character.

Prepare well for the firing conversation. Do not waver. Be very concise. It is never a good idea to try to explain the failure. The person being fired will rarely accept the explanation. They want to argue, to justify themselves. Tell the failing direct report he is not meeting expectations and that the organization is making a change. Don't allow second-guessing or negotiating a different outcome.

Deliver the firing message with empathy and firmness. Assure the fired person that contracts will be honored and severance pay and benefits will be provided. If appropriate, offer outplacement assistance. The manner in which a fired person departs the organization is subject to good judgment. In some cases, the fired person should have the opportunity to say goodbye to colleagues and collect his belongings with dignity. Never have security escort fired people from the workplace. That horrible image does far more damage to those who remain than the one who departs.

Masterful leaders take great care to immediately communicate with the fired person's staff. While the exact nature of the termination cannot usually be shared, use this moment to focus on the future. Communicate about interim leadership arrangements and reassure staff about timelines for future recruitment. Allow fired people to exit with grace and dignity if possible. Firing on a Friday makes it awkward to communicate with the fired person's staff. The weekend most certainly will give rise to destructive rumors. Fire on a Monday, and take the rest of the week to communicate. Move on, and help the staff to move on, too.

Can anything positive come from a firing? Absolutely. Learn from diagnosing what went wrong. Make adjustments to ensure that whatever went wrong becomes a leadership lesson for the future. Masterful leaders learn from their people mistakes. They rarely repeat them.

Firing Fiasco

As a newly promoted vice president with multiple department directors reporting to me, I thought I had arrived. I soon discovered that the dietary department director had been stealing food for personal use and resale. I waited until 5:00 p.m. Friday and fired him, assuming the assistant director could take over on Monday. I made no effort to inform the staff about the firing, again assuming I would pick up the pieces Monday morning. Over the weekend, the fired director called many staff members and told them he had been wrongfully accused. On Monday morning the assistant director turned in his resignation, and I was presented with a petition from the staff demanding the reinstatement of the director. When I did not comply, six out of thirty staff members quit on the spot. I spent the next thee months filling in for the food service director and putting together a new management team. This humbling learning experience marked an inglorious start to my career as a vice president.

Chapter 21: Number Two

Serving as "number two" can be the best of jobs or the worst of jobs. Being number two for a masterful leader and mentor is the best of all worlds. Learning leadership skills from a masterful leader is the best possible preparation for being a great chief executive officer someday. On the other hand, serving as number two for a selfish and narcissistic leader who claims all the credit for success and accepts none of the blame for failure is the worst of jobs.

1. **Select the best and brightest number two.**

2. **Mentor your number two.**

3. **Move your number two up or out when he is ready.**

Why do leaders even need a number two? First, for continuity in the event of a catastrophe. While most leaders aren't hit by a bus, they do die of heart attacks, cancer, and in accidents. They also occasionally melt down and get fired for personal indiscretions or bad professional conduct. When the unexpected occurs, the organization is better prepared to cope if a good number two is in place to pick up the leadership reins. This is as true for a department director as it is for the chief executive.

Mentoring a capable number two is part of every leader's responsibility. Masterful leaders are never threatened by strong number twos. On the contrary, they seek to create the strongest possible number two as a positive reflection of their leadership. That's what CEO Roberto Goizueta did at Coca Cola, preparing the company for a seamless transition when he passed away unexpectedly of cancer.

What makes a great number two? Leaders who share the number one's values and expectations, who are hard working and extraordinarily good at executing. Number twos who are interested in advancing the success of their number one are highly valued. Exceptional number twos never falter in their loyalty. The best number twos are ready to and capable of stepping into the number one job should circumstances require.

All leaders recognize that if they have been effective mentors, their number two will be ready to be number one someday. Masterful leaders anticipate the arrival of this moment. If promotion opportunities exist in the organization, the number two is given the opportunity. If not, masterful leaders acknowledge the time has arrived and assist their number two with finding the right opportunity to thrive elsewhere as number one.

It takes great insight to recognize this moment. It takes even greater courage to act on the moment. Masterful leaders have both, and they have the foresight and fortitude to start the mentoring process over again by selecting their next number two.

Masterful Mentor

I once worked for a masterful leader. He was a great teacher and mentor. He gave me more and more responsibility and never punished me when I made mistakes, unless that is, he didn't think I learned something from the mistake. Eventually, I rose through the ranks and became number two in the organization. After three years, the CEO sat me down for a profoundly important talk. "You have gone as far as you can go here. You are in your early 30s and I am in my early 40s. I'm not going anywhere soon." He went on to tell me I was ready to be a CEO, and over the next year he provided job search guidance and references as I interviewed for CEO positions. Eventually, I was hired to be the CEO of a troubled hospital. I was ready for the challenge, in no small part because of the insights and leadership wisdom I received from this masterful mentor.

Chapter 22: Direct Reports

Direct-report subordinates are a reflection of the leader. Select and retain only the best and brightest. Teach and mentor them and enable them to succeed personally and within the organization. Promote from within whenever possible. A leader surrounded by talented and well-mentored direct reports is likely to succeed. A leader surrounded by weak, ineffective, and disloyal direct reports is destined to fail.

1. **Select only the very best people for direct reports.**

2. **Teach and mentor them.**

3. **When vacancies occur, promote from within if possible.**

Masterful leaders give their direct reports quality time. Even the best can benefit from excellent direction, focused teaching, and mentoring. At a minimum, spend at least an hour a week of quality one-on-one time with each direct report. This time should be used for communicating direction and expectations, as well as listening and mentoring. Phone calls and e-mails are no substitute for one-on-one personal meetings.

Direct reports must absorb and practice the organization's values. Leaders effectively communicating the value system to them creates the corporate culture. The absence of such communication ensures that corporate culture cannot thrive. Constantly teach direct reports. Set expectations and reinforce the critical importance of accountability and delivering results. Masterful leaders always set a positive personal example for direct reports.

Retaining ineffective direct reports, or ones unable or unwilling to practice values and live the corporate culture, is a poor reflection on any leader. It communicates that you do not practice what you preach. This terminally affects leadership credibility. If you allow this to happen expect the worst possible consequences.

The importance of hiring quality direct reports begins at the department level. Department directors should select the best and brightest staff for their operations. Vice presidents should select and retain the best and brightest department directors. And likewise, chief executives must select and retain only the best COOs and vice presidents. Effective mentoring enables the best organizations to promote from within when leadership vacancies occur, a hallmark of quality organizations.

Chapter 23: Micro- and Macromanagement

Micromanagement has a bad reputation. Practitioners of micromanagement are said to be overbearing, or even worse, dictators. Micromanagers tell their subordinates what to do, when to do it, and what color to do it in. Details are important to them.

Micromanagement is not all bad. The passion to do things right, to exacting specifications, is often the driving force of micromanagers. On the other hand, micromanagers can be insecure. They may be inexperienced or may not know how to motivate, only how to give orders. Sometimes micromanagers have poor hiring skills and only select direct reports who are easy to intimidate. That is the negative side of micromanagement.

1. **Take an interest in details.**

2. **Don't apologize for attention to detail.**

3. **Vary your leadership style according to staff needs.**

On the other hand, macromanagers are hands off. They give overall direction and expect action and results. They don't interfere. They don't direct. They often don't pay much attention at all. Some leaders, chief executives and chief operating officers among them, are characterized as macromanagers. Some do this as a leadership strategy. Others are simply disengaged or lack the working knowledge to provide direction to direct reports.

Masterful leadership is a balance of applying micromanagement and macromanagement to achieve the best outcomes. When training and mentoring a new vice president or department director, micromanagement should be applied in the form of teaching and mentoring. Conversely, macromanagement may be the best strategy for a highly seasoned direct report. Most leaders have a diversity of direct reports, ranging from new and inexperienced to seasoned and highly capable. One leadership style does not fit all. Modulate between micro- and macromanagement as the situation and direct reports require.

A leader who practices in only one dimension, either micro- or macromanagement, is not likely to achieve great success. Study your situation and direct reports and dial up the approach best suited to achieving positive outcomes.

Insightful Leadership Change

A highly successful CEO was a believer in hands off macromanagement. His hospital was exceptional: great financial, quality, and service metrics for two decades. Then it started to slip. The CEO examined his leadership style and determined that the problem started with him. His subordinates proudly declared one of the best things about the CEO was that he was not a "micromanager." Indeed he was not. However, he discovered that his direct reports were not executing and achieving results. In fact, his subordinates were proud that they were not micromanagers either. The entire organization was populated with hands-off leaders. When the competition got stiffer and finances got tighter, the hospital's performance suffered. It got back on track when the CEO started modifying his leadership style. He remained a macromanager where appropriate and became a fearless micromanager when the situation demanded. Successful metrics quickly returned and the CEO announced proudly that "You can teach an old dog new tricks. I'm living proof."

Chapter 24: Setting an Exemplary Example

The chief executive is the chief example setter in any organization. Vice presidents are the leadership example setters for the departments under their responsibility. Physician department chairs set the example for physicians under their service. Department directors set the example for the supervisors and employees in their departments.

1. **Be optimistic. Always.**

2. **Park in the staff lot.**

3. **Use your expense account as if it will be published in the newspaper.**

One of the things new leaders sometimes fail to grasp is how closely they are observed and how powerful their example is. Staff take their cues from their department directors. Directors take their cues from senior management. Physicians take their cues from department chairs and chief medical officers. Masterful leaders embrace the power of positive example and cautiously avoid the danger of negative example. They appreciate enthusiasm, optimism, and a gung-ho attitude and instill these attributes in everyone around them.

Symbols present opportunities to set an exemplary example. Think about parking as a symbol. Some leaders use an assigned parking space next to the entrance. Others, knowing the power of symbolism, park in the staff lot and enter the building with the rank and file. This sets an excellent example and provides the leader with excellent employee connectivity opportunities every day.

Balance professional and personal life. Set a great work ethic example for direct reports. Lesser leaders work 40-hour weeks and are nowhere to be found on Friday afternoon. They never appear on the weekends or in the evening. Masterful leaders set an exemplary example of work ethic by occasionally being present at all hours and engaging the staff.

Some leaders are squeaky clean when it comes to setting the example for expense accounts. Those leaders spend their organization's funds responsibly and with great care. Executives with less character take advantage. They think nothing of buying a $200 bottle of wine at dinner, using a limo when a taxi would suffice, or purchasing extravagant gifts for subordinates they mistakenly think will be impressed.

Act as if your every move is observed and discussed by employees immediately. It probably is. Behave each day as if your activities will be featured on the evening news or tomorrow's morning paper. Use every opportunity to set an exemplary example, whether it is the way you conduct meetings, the way you talk with staff and physicians, or even the effort you make to stay connected with patients and families. The higher you rise in an organization, the more eyes are upon you. Masterful leaders understand this. They look for opportunities to set an exemplary example in everything they do.

Only the Best Will Do...For Me

One CEO set the worst possible example for his staff. He preached careful management of costs to employees and physicians, but he spent extravagantly on himself, his favorite subordinates, and his spouse and charged all of it to his hospital credit card. International travel, gourmet meals, expensive cigars and wine were all part of his spending ethic. He either did not know or did not care that his staff knew and talked about his excesses. Not surprisingly, his vice presidents all emulated the boss. Someday this CEO inevitably will embarrass his board when the local paper or TV station picks up the story of wasteful spending. Then, he'll be looking for a new position.

Chapter 25: Trusted Advisors

Leaders need trusted advisors. Why? As leaders rise in any organization hierarchy, it becomes increasingly difficult to get truly objective advice. Trusted outside advisors can provide a level of objectivity rarely or never available internally. Trusted advisors tell the truth.

1. **Find a trusted outside advisor.**

2. **Ignore resistance of your staff.**

3. **Always seek the truth.**

Every chief executive needs a safe sounding board for four key areas: strategy, senior leadership decisions, governance challenges, and finances. An independent point of view is invaluable. When selecting an outside advisor, wisdom in at least three of these key areas should be present in the advisor. Some leaders select several trusted advisors.

An effective trusted advisor has cumulative wisdom and provides that wisdom in ways that improve the leader's effectiveness. A trusted advisor can tell the leader when he is dead wrong or pursuing a wrongheaded strategy. A trusted advisor can help refine a leader's brainstorm into a highly effective and executable strategy.

A trusted advisor relationship is best when it is ongoing and longstanding. A trusted advisor can be far more effective when he is in continuous touch with the leader and is knowledgeable about current events, challenges, and opportunities. A trusted advisor relationship grows with time and can become extraordinarily effective. Not surprisingly, it is common for leaders to encounter resistance from their own staff regarding trusted outside advisors. Masterful leaders know that outside advisors can serve an invaluable purpose, even when their staff objects.

The choice to use an outside trusted advisor in no way undermines the importance of the leader's spouse, board chair, or trusted direct reports. All of these relationships can yield trusted advice. However, they are not substitutes for the value of a truly objective advisor who can bring both truth and wisdom to bear at the appropriate moment. The best trusted advisors know the difference and which moment to apply truth and when to apply wisdom.

The use of a trusted outside advisor has been rare below the chief executive level. However, the concept of the trusted advisor is applicable to all levels of leadership and is now becoming more commonplace with vice presidents, chief operating officers, and other members of senior leadership.

High of Cost of Peace

A new chief executive of a major health system knew intuitively he needed a trusted advisor. A physician and board member, he was appointed to the CEO office upon the untimely death of his predecessor. He lacked the executive seasoning most system leaders acquire through years of progressively more responsible leadership positions. Soon after taking office, he retained an outside trusted advisor to provide leadership counsel, as well as mentoring and coaching. One senior staff member vehemently objected to the advisor's presence. The staff member was rude, obnoxious, and disrespectful to the advisor and even to the CEO. Not long after being retained, the advisor confronted the CEO over the senior staff member's behavior. The CEO defended the subordinate, desperately wanting to keep peace and harmony among his staff and avoid a confrontation with the strong-willed subordinate. The advisor resigned, believing he could not effectively counsel the CEO. Less than one year later, the CEO and the obnoxious staff member were both let go by the board. It was a high price for the CEO to pay for such short-lived peace and harmony.

PHYSICIANS IN LEADERSHIP

Healthcare organizations have a unique opportunity to create profoundly important leadership synergies between executive leaders and physician leaders. In the first half of the 20th century, physicians usually led hospitals. In the second half of the century, professional executives assumed leadership of most hospitals. As the 21st century unfolds, integrating executive and physician leadership skills into new organization structures will ultimately achieve the best clinical and business results for hospitals and healthcare systems. Creating these new structures will take foresight, courage, and creativity. As the clinical and business complexities of hospitals and healthcare systems evolve, masterful leaders see a future of engagement and collaboration with physicians. Less enlightened leaders will obsess about competing with physicians for diminishing healthcare dollars. Masterful leaders will bring physicians into their leadership teams and create pathways to collaborate, not compete, with their medical staffs. Success begins with engagement.

Chapter 26: Engaging the Medical Staff

Engaging the medical staff in strategy and operations creates powerful physician allies and has been the genesis of advances in patient care, quality, and safety, as well as improved bottom lines. On the other hand, some leaders are concerned that the medical staff of today will be the competitors of tomorrow. Engagement can eliminate this unpleasant potential.

1. **Be open to physician engagement.**

2. **Personally attend key physician meetings. Be fully present and participate.**

3. **Never, ever lie to or mislead the medical staff.**

Engaging the medical staff should be a way of life for leadership at all levels. Department directors should engage the physicians in their departments. They should invite physicians to participate in key decisions and ensure that physicians are included in department staff meetings. Department directors likewise should attend and participate at medical staff meetings involving their areas of responsibility. Vice presidents should attend medical staff meetings for all areas of their responsibility. They should personally engage physicians in key decisions and actively solicit physician opinions when evaluating clinical quality, technology, and customer service initiatives.

CEOs need to be personally present at monthly meetings, such as the medical executive committee, as a symbol of engagement. Absences at medical executive or other key physician meetings such as quality and credentials committees do not go unnoticed by the medical staff. Being present but spending time texting or e-mailing is worse than being absent. The medical executive committee is one avenue for key leadership physicians to ask questions and give input to senior administrative staff. Physicians ask very direct questions and expect direct, honest answers.

Masterful leaders appreciate that the art of engaging the medical staff offers many opportunities for connectivity. Some leaders form physician advisory groups separate from the medical executive committee and other formal committees. Groups such as this can be excellent forums not only to evaluate potential future strategies but to learn how both the community and the medical staff may work collaboratively for the benefit of the organization and patients.

Many other opportunities for physician engagement exist, such as service line leadership, developing strategic plans, arranging contracts for hospital-based physicians, developing marketing plans, and joining the governing board, to name a few. Physician engagement at all levels is good for patient care and brings unique benefits to healthcare leadership at every level from individual clinical departments to the boardroom.

Chapter 27: Unique Benefits of Physician Leaders

Physicians are trained to think differently from business school-educated executives. These differences create unique opportunities for healthcare leadership. Medical school, residency, and fellowship programs teach physicians to be the "captain of the ship" when caring for patients. Physicians are encouraged to question the status quo, critically evaluate data and publications, and adopt new methods and treatments that benefit patients. Physicians share knowledge easily with their peers. Executive leaders would do well to emulate this practice.

1. **Use physician leaders to bring urgency to decision making.**

2. **Be open to physicians' unique problem-solving skills.**

3. **Engage physician leaders to be effective "translators."**

Years of clinical practice develop characteristics consistent with the physician's chosen specialty; for example: successful pathologists value order and methodology; surgeons are trained to fix problems; internists make decisions based on defined data points; emergency medicine physicians make decisions based on minimal data and rapidly change treatment plans as more information becomes available; anesthesia training is all about having a plan, expecting the unexpected, and managing risk.

Physicians are oriented to problem identification, investigation, problem solving, and then repeating this process with the next patient. These skills translate well into the executive suite. Physician leaders bring a sense of urgency. It is not in a physician's nature to spend an hour discussing a situation and then end a meeting without a definitive plan. Leadership teams can benefit from physicians' presence to speed up decision-making. Physician leaders also problem-solve differently from other members of the administrative team due to their unique training, often leading to creative ideas and strategies not previously considered.

Physicians can serve as effective conduits to the medical staff. Successful physician leaders serve as "universal translators" between administration and the medical staff. They are able to present decisions, strategies, and even disappointing news in a style that the medical staff can fully understand and appreciate. Masterful leaders are not just open to engaging physician leaders. They make it a very high priority.

Chapter 28: New Leadership Models

Average healthcare leaders think in terms of getting along with physicians. Masterful leaders value physicians and blend physicians' unique talents into their organization's leadership structure.

1. **Bring physicians into the executive suite.**

2. **Treat physicians as partners.**

3. **Respect physicians' patient care perspective.**

Share leadership responsibilities with physicians. There is value in physicians' unique decision-making and judgment skills that executive leaders do not always possess. Instead of subordinating those skills, embrace them. Arrange organization structures to include physicians as partners.

Combining executive leadership skills and physician leadership skills creates the most powerful healthcare enterprise leadership structure imaginable. True blending of these powerful skill sets will always outperform leadership structures populated exclusively by executives alone.

It is ironic that so few physician leaders occupy positions of real influence in the executive suites of healthcare organizations. Yes, there are some physician CEOs, but as a percentage of the total, it is a very small number. Some traditional healthcare administrators are afraid of physicians. But physicians are much closer to patient care than any executive can ever hope to be. Physicians understand good clinical quality vs. bad. They want the very best for patients, and their insights are invaluable to a progressive organization's leadership.

Traditional leadership structures usually include only one physician senior executive position, the chief medical officer (CMO). Masterful leaders work hard to include 30% - 40% physicians into their leadership structures. These structures enable physicians to serve in capacities far beyond the CMO position. Physician leaders can excel in operational positions, quality positions, and even positions such as information technology and fund raising if given the opportunity.

Masterful leaders understand the true value of integrating physicians into their leadership structures. Once this level of collaboration is achieved, healthcare organizations are always better for it. Blending of executive business talents and physician leader patient care talents is the future of healthcare, but this exciting future brings with it unique challenges in recruiting physician leaders.

Paradigm Shift

I assumed the interim CEO position for a large and troubled teaching hospital system where finances were declining, market share was slipping, and employee and physician morale was abysmal. The leadership challenge was daunting. I quickly assessed senior management and listened carefully to physician leaders, and members of middle management. "Old, sick, and tired" pretty much summed up the consensus about senior management. In short order, I either retired or fired all but the excellent chief nursing officer. The question of what to do next loomed large. A distinguished physician leader dropped in one day and said, "Michael, the medical staff of this system wants to help. We are dedicated. We love this place. Just ask us."

From that conversation grew an idea to try a totally new leadership approach. Instead of bringing in executive "temps" from the outside, I decided to lead the system with an Office of the President model to include three physician leaders and myself. Nominations for the physician leader positions were solicited from the medical staff, and over 50 were received. Three were selected and the Office of the President became a reality. For 18 months, the four of us guided the system back to prosperity. Finances improved. Patient volumes increased. Physician and staff morale rose measurably.

This successful leadership model was predicated on two key values. The first value was that all four of us treated each other as equal partners. The second value was we all endeavored to be exceptional listeners. We listened to patients, staff, and physicians. We listened, and we acted on their ideas and the complaints. The Office of the President brought this troubled healthcare system back to life.

Chapter 29: Recruiting Physician Leaders

As healthcare leaders seek to engage physicians in leadership positions, unique recruiting challenges arise. How do healthcare leaders go about ensuring that leaders invited to join leadership teams are the right physicians?

1. **Recruit only the best physicians to join the leadership team.**

2. **Encourage the physician leader to maintain a part time clinical practice.**

3. **Invest in leadership coaching and mentoring for new physician leaders.**

Masterful leaders reject physicians who are destined to fail. End-of-career physicians who have lost their passion for medicine, but not for income, are poor choices to become leaders. Poorly performing clinicians, or physicians who have difficulty getting along with peers, staff, or administration are unlikely to succeed. Fortunately, healthcare organizations have many physicians who possess great leadership potential.

Physicians who are respected by their peers, staff, and members of the leadership team can be great candidates. Physicians who are passionate about clinical quality and the best customer service for patients make wonderful leaders. Physicians who are articulate and who can collaborate to achieve organization goals, not just personal goals, make ideal leaders. Physicians who appreciate that executive leaders can, by their actions and decisions, contribute to quality care just as physicians do, also make ideal leaders.

When a leadership vacancy occurs or new positions are created, masterful leaders encourage physicians to apply and to nominate physician colleagues. When a pool of physician candidates is assembled, the recruitment and selection decisions are like any other leadership recruitment, with some special added considerations.

When considering a physician leader's potential, evaluate the applicant's body of work for instances when the candidate volunteered time and services for the benefit of the organization. Expect to see a pattern of serving effectively on committees and task forces. Evaluate the physician's continuing education: does it indicate an interest in administration and management? Inquire within the leadership team to ascertain the substance of the conversations that they have had with the prospective physician leader. Have those conversations led to improving the health system and patient care quality? Speak with the chief nursing officer and the directors of the areas that interact most directly with the physician leadership candidate. Look for evidence of mentoring, team building, operational execution, and excellent communication skills.

Once senior leadership has identified a potential physician leader, consideration also needs to be given to whether the new physician leader will be able to continue to practice clinically. Encourage physician leaders to continue to practice on some level to remain connected to the medical staff and patient care. Some specialties such as emergency medicine, pathology, radiology, and anesthesia lend themselves to part-time clinical practice in conjunction with a leadership position. If the physician being recruited has an office-based practice, such as surgery, family practice, internal medicine, or OB/GYN, continuing to practice is more challenging but no less important. Masterful leaders make accommodations for physician leaders to enable them to continue practicing.

> ### *Physician Leadership Innovation*
>
> *The CEO of a highly successful community hospital contemplated strategies on how to take his organization to the next level. He chose a very creative and enlightened leadership model. He added three physicians to his six-person administrative staff. Nominations were solicited from the medical staff and formal interviews were conducted to screen potential candidates. Three new physician leaders were selected to become Chairman of Clinical Quality, Tertiary Care Development, and Primary Care Development. Physician leaders were paired with administrative staff counterparts, creating a dyad leadership structure. Intensive focus and a completely new set of perspectives were brought to the administrative table in the areas of quality, tertiary care, and primary care by this leadership model of the future. A highly respected physician leadership coach was retained to mentor the new physician leaders, all of whom maintained part-time clinical practices.*

Chapter 30: Mentoring Physician Leaders

Masterful leaders do not stop with recruiting physician leaders into their team. They recognize teaching and mentoring are keys to long-term success. Physician leaders present unique challenges and unique opportunities for teaching and mentoring.

1. **Plan on "catch up" mentoring for new physician leaders.**

2. **Provide frequent and candid feedback.**

3. **Retain an experienced leadership coach for new physician leaders.**

Masterful leaders understand and appreciate that physicians bring special talents to their leadership responsibilities. On the other hand they also experience some special "catch up" needs. A mid-career executive who ascends to a level of vice president usually has a number of years to make and learn from mistakes in leading people. A new physician leader who ascends from clinical practice to a vice president level position lacks the years of seasoning and insights that making mistakes and learning from them brings. How does the physician leader gain these insights?

Masterful leaders ensure that new physician leaders are mentored and coached. Ideally, they personally impart their cumulative leadership wisdom to new physician leaders. Teaching and mentoring direct reports is never so vital as it is with new physician leaders. There are excellent physician leadership education professional associations to further the physician leader's knowledge base. There are also highly skilled physician leadership coaches who focus their teaching talents on assisting new physician leaders. In addition, there are specialized MBA programs available to physicians. While useful, however, academic programs are no substitute for an interested mentor and an experienced physician leadership coach.

Physician leaders also benefit from constant and candid feedback. Practicing physicians get daily feedback, most of it positive, from their patients. New physician leaders are sometimes discouraged by the lack of positive feedback. Care should be taken to ensure that new physician leaders receive all the candid feedback they need to reinforce skills and polish their leadership judgment.

Masterful leaders understand that physician leaders bring with them complementary skills. They also are sensitive to the need to supplement these skills with intensive leadership mentoring.

Chapter 31: Pitfalls for Physician Leaders

Becoming a masterful physician leader requires periodic evaluation of strengths, weaknesses, and potential blind spots. This can be accomplished through a combination of introspection, coaching, and mentoring, as well as developing relationships with individuals who are comfortable in giving truthful feedback. For physician leaders, there are some unique pitfalls to consider.

1. **Avoid the temptation to "do it all" yourself.**

2. **Don't be a "know it all."**

3. **Stay connected to patients.**

New physician leaders often find the concept of delegation challenging. Medical training centers around personal responsibility for patient care. As medical students and residents, physicians are taught to verify all physical findings via their own examination of the patient before making clinical decisions. Physicians can only bill for the treatment and procedures that they personally performed. Delegation is unacceptable.

Contrast this with how a successful executive leader functions. Executives must build a good team and trust direct reports to function at a high level. "Trust but verify" is the way leaders function. Direct reports are delegated the work for which a leader is held accountable. This dichotomy can place the physician leader in an uncomfortable position between the inclination to do everything himself and the need to delegate as a leader. This potential pitfall can be positively affected through coaching and mentoring. If the physician leader continues practicing medicine, he will repeatedly go from the clinical mindset to the leadership mindset, another unique challenge.

If there is only one physician on the organization's leadership team, team members may make the assumption that the physician is knowledgeable in all areas of medicine. This conjecture can be quite seductive as physicians are trained to take pride in being recognized as experts. It is important for physician leaders to confine opinions to their areas of true personal expertise. One of the most valuable assets of a physician leader can be realizing when other physicians' expertise and counsel is required to effectively guide the enterprise.

What happens if the physician's transition to leadership doesn't work? Despite best intentions, there is always the possibility that the physician will fail in the transition from clinical practice to physician leader. Not only might this result in resentment from the physician, the organization may end up losing an excellent clinical practitioner and lose credibility with the medical staff if the transition back to clinical practice goes poorly. A contingency plan for assisting the physician transition back into full-time clinical practice is highly advisable.

It is imperative for physician leaders to schedule time every week to interact with the medical staff, not only in the lunchroom or in meetings, but also in the workplace. Get into the exam rooms, the operating rooms, the nursing units, and diagnostic departments like laboratory and radiology. Spend a few hours in the emergency department and see how the hospital's front door is functioning. Masterful physician leaders get connected and stay connected to colleagues and patients.

Never Again

One of the hospital's most revered primary care physicians was recruited by administration to become the Vice President of Quality. His patient care skills and professional integrity were above reproach. At the time of his recruitment, no one considered what would happen if the new position did not work out. Unfortunately, over the next few months it became clear that the physician was not well suited to function in this leadership position. He was very effective at identifying physician-related quality problems. However, he proved to be absolutely incapable of counseling the problem physician about quality issues. When the chief medical officer concluded the physician leader had to step down, he was angry and humiliated; so much so that he left the hospital and set up practice at the competing hospital across town. He remained angry for years. This very unfortunate situation could have been avoided if a contingency plan had been put in place at the time of the physician's recruitment to leadership.

Chapter 32: Balance as a Physician Leader

It is difficult for any leader to strike an effective balance between work, family, and personal time. It is doubly difficult for physician leaders. Staying clinically active adds a significant additional time commitment to the workday. The physician's patients and peers, as well as the state licensing boards and national specialty boards, have the same expectations for all practicing physicians, including physicians with leadership responsibilities. Fulfilling those expectations takes time--lots of time.

1. **Know when to go home.**

2. **Manage time so that both clinical and leadership duties can be fulfilled.**

3. **Take pride in leadership work, even if positive feedback is minimal.**

Physicians are required to stay abreast of current literature and obtain required continuing medical education credits. For physician practices that involve procedures, there is no substitute for doing the work. Even physicians who work full time clinically tend to feel "rusty" after a two-week vacation. The challenge is immense for physician leaders who also practice clinically and continue to do procedures. In addition to maintenance of medical professional standards, physician leaders must also remain current with the literature pertaining to healthcare organizations.

Another huge challenge, especially for new physician leaders, is recognizing when it is time to go home. In clinical practice, the workday finishes when the last office patient is seen, the last inpatient is rounded on, the last case is completed, or the last hour in a clinical shift arrives. Clinical days have a defined beginning and end. As a physician leader, there is always more that can be done that day. Assistants tend to keep the entire day's schedule filled with appointments and meetings. Only by having discipline in scheduling and time management can a physician leader expect to achieve balance between work and personal needs.

Another confusing aspect of life for new physician leaders is learning to take pride in non-clinical work. In practice, patients say "thank you" multiple times a day. This immediate and frequent positive feedback becomes very gratifying, even addictive. Every day, clinical physicians drive home knowing that a patient's lifestyle improved, a dying patient was saved, or a grieving family was comforted. Loss of positive patient feedback can, if unrecognized, be the impetus for a physician leader to consider giving up on becoming a physician leader. Unlike patient care, the results of non-clinical leadership work may take months or years to come to fruition. The higher up on the organizational ladder a leader climbs, the fewer people there are to give positive feedback. It is imperative for physician leaders to find ways to take pride in the intrinsic value of leadership work.

VALUES IN LEADERSHIP

Organizations do not have values. People have values. People reflect the values of their leaders. Leaders establish and set the personal example for values. Successful organizations have leaders with great values and people within who adopt and live those values. Underperforming organizations have leaders with poor values or no values at all. The actions of every member of the staff reflect the values of their leader. Values require a moral compass and courage to live by that compass. Leaders need life balance and occasional solitude to see where their compass is pointing and who is accomplishing the outcomes needed for success, and who is merely appearing to work hard. Masterful leaders have character and act with integrity. Always.

Chapter 33: Moral Compass

"Once in a while you will stumble upon the truth, but most of us manage to pick ourselves up and hurry along as if nothing had happened."
Winston Churchill

Leaders are the needle for the organization's moral compass. That compass can be rock steady, or it can waver and spin like a trip through the Bermuda Triangle. The CEO sets the course by which all members of the organization steer. Every leader in the organization has moral compass responsibility for the areas and people under their direction.

1. **Follow your moral compass.**

2. **Expect direct reports to have the same level of integrity as you.**

3. **Fire anyone who lacks integrity.**

Set the example for integrity. Masterful leaders create the value system of the organization and create the culture for living those values. There can be no compromise in reading the moral compass. In every good organization, right can be distinguished from wrong. The CEO and every leader under his responsibility show the organization by their actions how to lead within the ethical or moral guidelines set forth in the organization's culture. There can be no cheating where the moral compass is concerned.

The absence of a moral compass is profoundly felt. If the director of a department lacks a moral compass, every one of the department's employees will know. The effect will be compromises in attitude, service, and quality. If a vice president lacks a moral compass, an entire division will be affected. If a CEO lacks a moral compass, other leaders will lack the fortitude to do the right thing for employees, physicians, and, sadly, for patients.

History is full of examples of organizations and leaders who lost their way. It takes great courage and discipline to lead and live within a culture of integrity. It takes character. Enron, Worldcom, and Arthur Andersen famously lost their way due to a lack of integrity. Their leaders cheated, got caught, and went down. Some went to jail. All ended up in disgrace. They either never had or lost their moral compass. Hospitals and healthcare systems have their own disgraceful examples where the moral compass was missing or not followed.

One sensitive area where leaders have their moral compasses tested relates to impaired staff and physicians. Employees and physicians in healthcare organizations have access to drugs that can be very tempting and there are numerous examples of drug and alcohol impaired staff and physicians. Other forms of impairment are mental health problems and age-related mental impairment. Masterful leaders never, ever compromise patient care when impairment is discovered. The affected physician or staff member is removed immediately until successful treatment is completed. If that is not possible, the staff member or physician must leave--no compromises.

Act as if your every decision will be judged by the moral compass. Expense accounts, hiring and firing decisions, competitive strategies will all someday be judged and compared to the moral compass. There can be no small diversions from right or wrong. Take personal accountability for all your decisions.

Poor leaders believe they can compromise and never be caught. They are profoundly wrong. Leaders who ignore moral compass responsibility always pay a price. So, too, do their organizations. Redemption is not an option when a leader lacks integrity. There are no second chances. Resignation or termination are the only options for leaders who lie, cheat, steal, or otherwise lead their organizations astray. Eventually, these leaders always get caught and deserve the consequences of their actions.

Missing Compass

A physician leader was known to be an exceptional clinician. He rose through the leadership hierarchy like a rocket and eventually became chief operating officer of a respected specialty hospital. According to many of his staff, however, he lacked any kind of moral compass. He spent lavishly on his hospital expense account and engaged in favoritism among certain pet associates. He employed family members in questionable consulting assignments and ignored conflict of interest policies. He engaged in activities that created a hostile work environment. He hired attractive young ladies with no visible duties or skills and fired anyone who questioned his decisions. The worst part of this story is that his CEO boss knew about these transgressions and chose to ignore them. It is only a matter of time before an insider blows the whistle—on both of them.

Chapter 34: Courage

It takes courage to be a masterful leader. Leaders make decisions every single day. Some are easy. Some are hard. In a turnaround, hard decisions come at you like a tsunami, every day. But there are singularly important decisions that define a leader. These are the decisions that take more than analytical skill. They take courage.

1. **Make the right decision, not the easy decision.**

2. **Never compromise your values.**

3. **When making really tough decisions, look in the mirror for guidance.**

Have the courage to make the best decisions, not just the easiest decisions. The average leader looks for "cover" and a way out when confronted with tough decisions. What do you do when a revered physician starts to slip due to advancing age? Masterful leaders ensure that the physician is graciously retired from practice, even if the physician desperately wants to delay the inevitable. The average leader looks for excuses to allow the physician to continue to practice. Until, that is, a patient is harmed. When lawsuits are filed and bad publicity erupts, average leaders finally act.

What does a CEO do when a board member has an inappropriate personal relationship with his vice president of nursing? The average CEO looks the other way. The masterful CEO has the courage to confront both parties. To do otherwise compromises the organization's culture. A moral compass in good order is a necessary prerequisite for this kind of courage.

What do you do when financial performance lags and no one seems to be alarmed? Show courage in the face of passive acceptance of declining performance. Accept responsibility and mobilize the organization to improve. No excuses. Masterful leaders have the courage to improve, even if no one else seems to care.

Every decision has both positive and negative consequences. Some people will be happy with a decision. Some will be upset. It takes courage to make a decision when you know that most people, or perhaps everyone, will be upset with the decision. A leader may not look for controversy, but should not be afraid of it either.

Masterful leaders are the cumulative result of all the courageous decisions of their career. They are less afraid of failure than they are of failing to show courage in the face of adversity.

Battle of the Brain Surgeons

A group of three physician specialists were the only option for community residents and the sole community hospital. They decided not to accept or care for Medicaid patients, Blue Cross patients, and patients too poor to have any source of payment. They only covered the hospital emergency room four days a week. On the other days, patients were faced with a one-hour drive or ambulance transport.

The hospital's CEO tried in vain to convince the group to recruit new members, to care for the poor, and take emergency call seven days a week. After a year of unsuccessful attempts, he began the search for two new specialists. The group mounted a vicious campaign to get the CEO fired. They lobbied board members tirelessly in church, at the country club, and every imaginable social setting. The board began to waver, but the CEO never flinched. He reminded the board that the hospital was for all the community, not just the people who had insurance coverage acceptable to the three specialists.

The CEO persevered in doing the right thing, knowing he might lose his job over this battle. He eventually succeeded in recruiting new physicians, making coverage available for all residents. The three specialists never gave up their relentless quest to have the CEO dismissed. If awards were given for courage in healthcare, this CEO would receive the medal of honor.

Chapter 35: Power

Masterful exercise of power: we all aspire to it, but only the most capable leaders know it is important and how to do it. Remaining leaders, unfortunately, exercise power with anything but mastery.

Power, exercised properly, can bring people and organizations to new heights. Power can also destroy people and organizations. Where is the dividing line between power exercised properly and power used as a destructive force? The answer lies in the understanding of the different kinds of power and how they are combined into leadership.

1. **Use power very sparingly.**

2. **Monitor and teach subordinates, don't order them.**

3. **Never abuse power or tolerate anyone who does.**

Position power comes with the office. It begins with first level supervisors and reaches its zenith in the office of the chief executive. Influence is another form of power. It comes not from position, but from the ability to change the behavior of others. Inspiration is a form of power too; like influence, but on a greater order of magnitude. To inspire is to wield enormous power. The ability to teach is the ultimate form of power. The ability to influence and inspire others is to be able to teach them.

New leaders often use position power alone. In a single department, position power may suffice for a department director, for a time. As leaders mature, the best learn to use influence as power. More gifted leaders eventually learn to inspire. Masterful leaders learn to combine position power, influence, inspiration, and teaching to develop highly effective leaders and build exceptional organizations.

There is profound danger in power. It can be used and abused in a hundred different ways. It can be used to intimidate. It can be used to cause others to cower and do things they would never do unless forced by abusers of power. Abuse of power is almost always obvious. The abuser is a bully, a narcissist, a cheat. Abusers almost always end up failing. Falling out of power may mean loss of position, loss of prestige, and a few even end up losing their freedom and enter prison for extended stays. Every one of these power abusers deserves what they get.

The best practitioners of power are quiet, humble, and dignified. They influence. They inspire. They teach. They understand exercise of power is an art, and its effective use for the good of an enterprise is masterful leadership.

Dignified Power

After 35 years in the same medical center, the CEO was the epitome of the best exercise of power. He literally grew up in the organization, starting as a department director and progressing up the ranks over 20 years to become CEO. He never used position power. He was a great practitioner of influence power. He also was an excellent teacher, leading by setting a wonderful example. He was gifted at inspiring staff and physicians to do their best. He was quiet, humble, and dignified throughout his career. He used his extraordinary power to build his hospital from a 100-bed community hospital to one of the largest (600 beds) tertiary teaching hospitals in the state. People followed this masterful leader because they believed in the direction that he set for the future--and what a future it turned out to be.

Chapter 36: Effort vs. Outcome

We are all capable of effort. Fewer of us are capable of achieving good outcomes. The distance between effort and outcome is sometimes enormous. Masterful leaders bridge that distance without conscious thought.

1. **Know what outcomes must be achieved.**

2. **Verify that the outcomes are actually achieved.**

3. **Check back periodically to verify outcomes are sustained.**

Even experienced leaders can be fooled into thinking that effort always achieves outcomes. Assembling a team and charging it with achieving a specific outcome, say reducing room turnaround time in a busy surgery department, is only half the battle. The team must find workable solutions and implement them successfully. Verifying later that turnaround time reductions have actually been accomplished and sustained is the desired outcome. Some leaders think they are done after the assignment to fix the problem is made. Still others think they are done when the mission is reported accomplished. Masterful leaders know that checking back to see that the solution is actually working and the outcome is sustained is essential.

You are measured by the outcomes you achieve. Insist that those reporting to you achieve outcomes too. Expenditure of effort, while worthy of note, is not sufficient to move an organization ahead. Expenditure of effort alone will not change behavior, and it will not produce positive financial or clinical quality results. Only careful identification of desired outcomes and follow-up to see that those outcomes are achieved will produce desired positive results.

Appreciate that outcomes achieved are rarely permanent. Fixing a patient throughput problem in the emergency room is a positive outcome. But, the fix may be fleeting. Staff turnover, physician changes, IT system updates--all may conspire to have the fix atrophy over time. Constantly be on guard for checking and rechecking to ensure that actions achieved are sustained. When performance slips, act again to identify and fix the contributing problems.

Learning the difference between effort and outcome takes experience and common sense. Masterful leaders understand the difference and never settle for effort alone.

All Talk, No Results

A chief medical officer became very frustrated over a period of two years spent trying to get the emergency medicine chief to deal with patient waiting time and customer service problems. According to Press Ganey service scores, the emergency department's overall ranking was in the 10th percentile, nothing short of abysmal. The emergency medicine chief made one promise after another to the CMO. He said he was making great efforts to fix the problems and outlined potential solutions he was "trying hard" to implement. After two years, no real progress had been made. Finally a board member's neighbor complained bitterly about waiting time and poor service in the emergency room. The board convened a special meeting during which the CEO and CMO were both admonished for lack of outcome in resolving the longstanding problems. All three leaders gained valuable insight into the difference between efforts and outcomes from this humbling experience.

Chapter 37: Bad Behavior

Healthcare organizations bring out the best in people. Most of the time. On occasion, they bring out the very worst. Physicians, employees, and members of leadership are not immune. In other organizations, bad behavior leads to poor customer service, lost business, and damaged reputations. In healthcare organizations, bad behavior leads to all of these things; but in addition, bad behavior also can harm patients.

1. **Never tolerate bad behavior.**

2. **Never retain subordinates who tolerate bad behavior.**

3. **Assume all bad behaviors will be made public someday soon.**

Every healthcare organization has a unique culture. One measure of culture is leadership tolerance for bad behavior. Some organizations have a very high tolerance for bad behavior. These are the places where physicians berate the staff in front of patients and other employees. These are the places where board members bully their way into operating decisions. And these are places where members of management act unprofessionally toward employees and get away with it.

Bad things happen in these organizations. Employees quit in disgust and file lawsuits. Patients get frustrated and take their business elsewhere. Talented physicians become disenchanted and move their practices to organizations with higher standards. Nothing good ever comes from leadership having a high tolerance of bad behavior. Bad behavior is visible proof of an organization's lack of character.

Bullying, obnoxious behavior, and any actions inconsistent with a professional atmosphere should never be tolerated. In excellent organizations, bad behavior gets reported and acted upon. Masterful leaders are willing to fire members of management, physicians, and even board members who exhibit bad behavior. Zero tolerance is present at every level of management, from front line supervisors to the chief executive's office in masterfully led organizations.

The level of tolerance for bad behavior is a barometer for the corporate culture. Masterful leaders and the excellent organizations they lead have very low tolerance for bad behavior. They create an environment where quality care and quality physicians and high staff morale thrive. These organizations never make excuses for bad behavior. They don't have to.

Sad, but True

Examples of bad leadership behavior are numerous. It is hard to select just one. Here are a few true one-liners:

- *Administrative staff takes delivery of new company cars during the week of staff layoffs.*

- *Vice president preaches following rules to his department directors but parks his car in the patient lot and cuts in line ahead of patients and staff in the cafeteria.*

- *Hospital CEO uses maintenance department staff to do home renovations. Also pays alimony out of hospital funds.*

- *CFO purchases $20 cigars with company credit card while at restaurant entertaining vendors. Later claims it's nobody's business how much he pays for cigars.*

- *System CEO sends romantic text messages to his administrative assistant during board meetings. Thinks no one notices.*

- *Board member ensures his own telecommunications company gets hospital contract by reviewing all other bids before submitting his.*

The list goes on.....

Chapter 38: Never Mess with the Help

The ultimate in bad behavior is having a sexual liaison with a subordinate at work. Many leaders have been dismissed for this behavior. Having an affair with a subordinate is just plain wrong. And yet, wrong or not, it is common and accepted in some healthcare organizations. The moral compass is nonexistent in these organizations. Anything goes.

1. **Never have an affair at work.**

2. **Do not tolerate anyone who does.**

3. **Assume organizations that tolerate a hostile work environment will be successfully sued.**

Leaders who engage in affairs with subordinates often think they are so clever that the affair is unnoticed around the organization. No one is that clever. When an affair is under way, everyone knows. If the CEO is the one having the affair, the hospital's culture and value system is compromised. At best, staff and physicians think the leader is a hypocrite. At worst, the leader is viewed with disdain. If a department director or vice president is having a workplace affair, it is likely that everyone in those areas knows about the affair except the offender's spouse.

Affairs may be one of the worst of the moral compass problems, but they are not the only one. Creating or accepting a hostile culture of off-color jokes, inappropriate touching, etc., is just as bad as having or condoning a workplace affair. Organizations that allow a hostile environment to continue should reread their own mission statement. It undoubtedly says something about dignity and justice in the workplace.

Make your expectations known on the subject of affairs and hostile work environments. Cover this subject when new direct reports are hired and periodically reinforce the message. Make it clear workplace affairs and engaging in practices that create an environment where any employee is made to feel uncomfortable are not tolerated. Ever.

Affairs never end well for either the people involved or the organization. Hard feelings are inevitable. Expensive lawsuits or settlements are commonplace and no one ever views the leaders in quite the same way following an affair or condoning of inappropriate behavior. Masterful leaders never mess with the help, and they don't tolerate anyone who does.

Profound Consequences

Leaders in a hospital with a busy and profitable cardiac surgery service line had multiple opportunities to demonstrate courage. None of them did. For years, heart surgeons created a work environment in the operating room that numerous staff members found offensive. Bad language was used. Female bottoms were pinched. Unwanted sexual invitations to staff members were everyday occurrences. Many leaders knew about these practices. The operating room director knew. Vice presidents knew. The chief medical officer knew and so did the chief executive. Instead of showing courage, they ignored the problems and the staff who reported the problems. The situation did not end well for the hospital when it lost a multimillion-dollar suit filed by a staff member who did not appreciate and complained about the sexually charged atmosphere in the operating room.

Chapter 39: Work/Life Balance

Masterful leaders have a life. A life outside of and beyond the organization they serve. Balanced people are the best leaders. Workaholics, those with no life beyond the organization's walls, can never be great leaders. Why? Because no subordinate can ever work as hard as a workaholic boss. Workaholic bosses are rarely effective delegators. Workaholics attempt and usually fail at doing their own work and the work of their direct reports too.

1. **Work hard. Play hard too.**

2. **Set a good work and life balance example for those around you.**

3. **Have fun.**

Masterful leaders are hard working. They may work a 12-hour day, or even a seven-day week on occasion. But no masterful leader always works 12-hour days or seven-day weeks. To do so leaves no time for a family, personal fulfillment, and a balanced life. A balanced life is a foundation for the best leaders. A leader with no interests or life outside work is not a good role model for direct reports. Even the most driven and obsessed leader needs a little down time and a little perspective. Having a life beyond the office walls leads to better decisions, better communication, and ultimately better leadership.

Show some discipline. Know how to turn off the phone and computer for quiet time and solitude. Not every e-mail or text must have an instant response. You do not have to be in constant contact 24/7 to be a masterful leader. On the contrary, be disciplined about down time.

Know how to have fun. Don't always run yourself and your direct reports into exhaustion. Surround yourself with people who have balance in their lives. They laugh. They enjoy the company of others. They have passion for work, but also for family, friends, and interests outside of work. They are not grim, pompous, or one-dimensional. They are well balanced.

Set cultural standards and performance expectations, not work hours. Watch for direct reports with workaholic tendencies. Counsel them and set a positive example for work, not obsession with work. Teach how to accomplish objectives, not 80-hour weeks. Model these values and teach them to your direct reports.

Chapter 40: Solitude

Time alone is vastly underrated. With the quest to be instantly available at all times, there is virtually no time for leaders to be alone. This is as true for front line supervisors as it is for chief executives. Making time to be alone takes discipline and appreciation of the value of solitude. Masterful leaders have both.

Leaders' time is consumed with meetings. In between meetings, the requirement to answer e-mails, texts, and correspondence can be all-encompassing. A leader's time is never his own. Or so goes common thinking. Make time to be alone. Leave the pressure of the office and go someplace comfortable to be alone. Solitude time is first and foremost time to think.

1. **Spend a little time in solitude every week.**

2. **Make time for thinking, not just doing.**

3. **Relax and recharge yourself regularly.**

Most of a leader's time is consumed with responding, not thinking. Responding is not leadership. Make time to think things through. Slow down and concentrate. What do you need to think about? People decisions: who to promote; who to develop further; who to fire. People decisions take quality time. Time alone to think about key people is vital to making sound decisions.

Envisioning the future is another thinking matter. Creating a future vision takes time and solitude. Planning major strategies and conceiving the initiatives that advance the organization take quality time. Reports and conferences are important, but quality time alone envisioning the future is important too. Leadership in its essence is solitary. Leaders alone make the hard decisions. Leaders are responsible and accountable for each and every one of these hard decisions.

Don't spend every waking moment working. Appreciate the value of relaxing. Sometimes relaxation is a group activity, as with family. Sometimes, however, a little solitary time, an opportunity to relax, refresh, and recharge, is valuable and necessary, too. Solitude leads to better decisions, better future plans, and, better, more balanced leadership. Masterful leaders spend time alone. It is one of their keys to success.

SYMBOLS OF LEADERSHIP

Leaders use symbols as multipliers of their value system. The best leaders teach by personal example. They understand and appreciate that the organization's eyes are always upon them. They don't hide. They don't resent these eyes. They relish the eyes and ears of the organization as teaching opportunities. If they want the organization's people to be nice to customers, leaders set the example by being nice to customers, and the people who care for customers. Leaders are accessible to both staff and customers. They relish contact and connectivity. Self-aware leaders recognize when their time is over and are able to leave with dignity. Masterful leaders leave behind an organization and people who are far better than they were when the leader arrived.

Chapter 41: Executive Assistants

Executive assistants are a window into the leader's character. Assistants should treat everyone they interact with as if the leader himself were the contact. Select, train, and treat assistants the way you want to be treated.

1. **Treat your assistant with the same respect as a family member.**

2. **Make sure your assistant is nice to everyone.**

3. **Realize your assistant is your two-way window to the organization.**

Never tolerate self-important, rude, or abusive assistants. On the contrary, such awful assistants are often the first warning sign that an ineffective leader can be found in the office behind the assistant.

"Imperious" is a word that unfortunately describes more than a few assistants to senior executives and CEOs. The presence of an imperious assistant is a leading indicator of a troubled corporate culture. A leader who tolerates an imperious assistant in his own office is highly unlikely to create and nurture a culture of customer service and responsiveness to a patient's problems and concerns.

Ensure that your executive assistant is unfailingly friendly to all comers, in person, on the phone, or in e-mails. Take great care to ensure that all people are treated with equal dignity. Requests are promptly answered, and all who seek counsel and your presence receive a quick answer. Assistants who are plugged into the organization grapevine can be very helpful to leaders who are open to all avenues of information to gauge the pulse of the staff. In this context, assistants can be excellent informal advisors to their leader.

One characteristic of a leader's assistant that must always be present, and never compromised, is office and personal confidentiality. You must have unconditional and complete trust that your assistant always maintains strict confidentiality. Confidentiality breaches, even small ones, must never be tolerated.

Executive assistants are the persons closest to the leader, literally and figuratively. Masterful leaders treat assistants with great respect. Invest in the assistant's professional development and ensure that the assistant is treated as an important member of the leadership team. This is as true for a department director's assistant as it is for the chief executive's executive assistant.

"Responsive" and "anticipatory": those words best describe the executive assistant to a masterful leader. Anything less in an assistant is the mark of a leader with much room for improvement.

Too Late for Anger Management

The CEO's assistant had survived three CEO changeovers over two decades. With each leadership change, the assistant became more imperious. He treated everyone with disdain, except the hospital's board members. Even the assistant's CEO boss was only grudgingly tolerated. Everyone else was treated like dirt. He was angry all the time. Other assistants in the executive suite were in constant turmoil, and not one of them was happy. The CEO and board retained me as a senior advisor to help the health system through a rough time. The CEO's assistant treated me with special disdain. Unfortunately for the assistant, the CEO stepped down and the board asked me to become interim CEO. I did, and my first act was to fire the CEO's miserable assistant. In the brief termination meeting, the tearful assistant volunteered to take an anger management course. I agreed that was an excellent idea and offered to pay for it instead of outplacement assistance.

Chapter 42: Office and Access

Masterful leaders locate their offices in close proximity to direct report subordinates. Informal communication opportunities are abundant when leaders see and are seen by their direct reports regularly. In an age where e-mail and text messages have become substitutes for human interaction, opportunities for face-to-face, personal contact are worth striving for.

1. **Stay close to your direct reports.**

2. **Personalize your office.**

3. **Delight a caller. Answer your own phone.**

While all leaders need privacy and solitude for thinking and planning, it is also important for staff and physicians to have informal access to their leaders on a regular basis. Executive assistants must not be an impediment to access. Blocking access to the leader will contribute to a perception that the leader is isolated. For leaders with multiple site responsibilities, it is highly advisable to have regular office hours at these locations. Regular personal presence encourages the relationship building that sporadic site visits can never achieve.

An unfortunate trend in hospitals and healthcare systems today is for office locations to be more and more isolated from customers, patients. Healthcare systems frequently create "corporate offices" in offsite locations where patient and physician contact is virtually impossible. Some hospitals also move their administrative staffs offsite, away from patients. Masterful leaders avoid this trend. They relish seeing patients, staff, and physicians on a daily basis.

The office itself is important, too, not just its location. The office is a window to your personality and an important symbolic opportunity. Offices should have at least a few personal effects, such as family photos and personal mementos. Sterile offices with no personal effects telegraph that you are a sterile person. Arrange your office so that you can sit with people you are addressing, not behind a desk. Leaders who always sit behind their desks are telegraphing that they are in charge, something secure leaders don't need to do. Offices can range from tidy to looking like a tornado aftermath. Tidy offices set a better example.

Answer your phone personally when the opportunity presents itself. Some masterful leaders make it a point to answer their phone for an hour a day to create a sense of immediate access. Far from being an imposition, masterful leaders see this as an opportunity to stay connected, much to the surprise and delight of callers.

Masterful leaders are willing to spend at least a little time with unscheduled visitors. These may be direct reports with urgent questions. It may be a physician with a complaint or a good idea. It may even be an employee with something important to say. Make sure your office is regularly open to these informal and unscheduled contacts. Not only is this valuable for staying connected, it is just good manners.

Mixed Message

A very successful hospital system's offices were housed in the system's main hospital. As the system grew, the CEO decided to move his office across the street. A new "corporate office" was born, cut off for all practical purposes from staff, physicians, and patients. As the system continued to grow and prosper, the CEO moved again, this time across town. A mahogany and marble edifice was created to house the CEO and his growing corporate staff of several hundred. Physicians, staff, and employees stopped complaining. They knew it was pointless. The corporate office was now so distant, it was completely disconnected. The sad irony of this office story is that the CEO was a gifted "people" person, who now rarely sees his people. Unfortunately, this office relocation story is a common one for healthcare systems.

Chapter 43: Good Manners

Good business manners are missing or much diminished in many healthcare enterprises. Yet, masterful leaders still endeavor to set a positive example for good manners as part of their personal value system. They are nice to people--all people, all of the time.

1. **Say "hello" to everyone, everywhere.**

2. **Thank people personally.**

3. **Listen to people in meetings. Don't allow multitasking.**

Be nice: a simple but effective formula for good manners. One small thing every leader can do is to greet everyone they see walking through the organization. The simple gesture of making eye contact and saying hello to everyone allows the leader to set the example for staff. If a director does this, his staff will follow the lead. If a vice president does this, his division's staff will follow. If a CEO does this, it sets the stage for a friendly corporate culture.

Another core tenet of good manners is responsiveness. Unanswered or ignored calls, letters or e-mails set a tone of poor manners. While every leader is deluged with requests and questions, it shows excellent responsiveness to answer each and every one, and on a timely basis.

"Thank you" gestures are a superb way to show good manners. Every healthcare leader is presented with numerous opportunities to use "thank you" gestures. E-mail is quick and convenient. Personal phone calls are always appreciated. Hand-written notes or cards are grand "thank you" gestures. Personal notes are so uncommon that when used they distinguish the sender in the most positive way.

Masterful leaders set a good example for direct reports and teach the importance of good manners. Leaders who tolerate bad manners in direct reports set a poor example. Demonstrate good manners through positive behaviors in meetings. Listening to the person or persons speaking in a meeting is a nearly forgotten expression of personal manners. It is far more common for leaders to check e-mails, send texts, or tweets, or even accept phone calls during meetings. While reinforcing their leader's self-importance, such behaviors are poor manners and set a poor example. Masterful leaders have unfailingly good manners. And so do the people around them.

Walmart Greeter-Friendly

I was struggling to improve the hospital's terrible reputation for unfriendly staff. Shortly after taking office as CEO, I conducted a first series of town hall meetings for all employees. During the meeting, I declared that from that day forward, employees would be required to make eye contact and say "hello" to everyone they encountered. Patients, family members, physicians, employees, and volunteers were all to be greeted. We may have been broke, but we could still be nice, I thought. Soon patients and family members began noticing that the hospital was now an extraordinarily friendly place. The simple gesture of our staff saying "hello," in the halls, in the parking lots, in patient rooms, in the cafeteria, and even the restrooms, had transformed the hospital's culture overnight. I knew we had succeeded when the local newspaper ran an editorial on how the hospital had become as friendly as Walmart.

Chapter 44: Taking Office

Every leader has a first day in office. Upwardly mobile leaders have many first days in office during a career. By the time a leader gets to the chief executive's suite, he may have experienced dozens of first days. A successful business executive once wryly remarked, "You're never as smart as you are in your first 90 days in office." Masterful leaders use their first days in office as learning and first impression opportunities.

1. **Listen to people first, before expressing your own opinion.**

2. **Paint the lobby.**

3. **Never trash your predecessor.**

Use your first days, weeks, and months to absorb a wide range of knowledge about your new responsibilities. Take time to meet and really get to know your new direct reports. Learn the process of the department, division, or enterprise, depending on the level of the leadership position. Get to know your customers. Customers may be patients, physicians, or staff, depending on your position. Masterful leaders always dedicate time for learning from their customers.

First days in office are opportunities to learn about the strengths and weaknesses of the new area of responsibility. Collectively, learning during the first days, weeks, and months provides a sense of history and creates a positive first impression with the staff. Understanding history is the first step of charting the future.

Use symbolism upon taking office. Do something positive that says, "A new leader is here." A new department director might fix up the employee break room. A chief nursing officer might recognize the nursing staff for their professionalism. A new CEO might purchase a long awaited item of clinical technology or paint the lobby. Positive symbols make taking office an opportunity to send a message that things are going to change, and for the better.

Unfortunately, some leaders don't take time to really learn their new area of responsibility upon taking office. Getting to know people, processes, and customers is not all that important to them. One of the most destructive things these new leaders do is trash their predecessor. Nothing the previous leader did measures up. Not the people. Not the processes. Not the outcomes. These kinds of new leaders rarely succeed with anything in their first days except demoralizing their new direct reports.

Masterful leaders go through their entire careers using first days in office as learning opportunities. When they have learned all they can, they move ahead--literally. They move their people ahead, their organization ahead, and inevitably they move themselves ahead.

Nothing Ventured, Nothing Gained

A physician chief operating officer used a powerful symbol in his first week in office. He was visited by one of his physician colleagues, a cardiologist who pleaded his case for replacement of an outdated cardiac monitoring system. The COO's predecessor had a reputation of "just say no" to physician requests. The new monitoring system had been requested and denied for four years running. By then, the existing system was down 50% of the time and maintenance and parts were difficult to obtain. Patients were inconvenienced. Diagnoses and treatments were delayed. So the cardiologist made one last pitch to the new COO. Surprisingly, the new COO said "yes," and the updated cardiac system was promptly delivered and installed. The "yes" decision created a positive sensation in the hospital. Physicians, long denied technology improvement requests, began coming forward again. Most of the time, the COO said "yes" and much needed clinical technology upgrades were made throughout the hospital. The symbolism of listening to physicians and saying "yes" whenever possible initiated a reinvigorated culture of the hospital, one that is still appreciated to this day.

Chapter 45: Leaving Office

We all leave office. At least once. Most leaders leave office many times in a career. Each departure is an opportunity to show grace and dignity. Good leaders use these opportunities wisely. Lesser leaders exit their office angry and disillusioned, leaving something behind--a lasting negative impression.

1. **Anticipate when it's time to go. Don't wait for somebody to push you.**

2. **Leave office as if you might come back someday.**

3. **Be nice on your way out.**

There are numerous circumstances of leaving office. You may move up in the same organization. You may leave the organization for a new challenge elsewhere. You may retire. Or you may be fired. Preceding any departure from office is the recognition that it is time for a change. Masterful leaders know when it is time to go, and have the fortitude to proactively arrange to exit when their time has come.

For self-aware leaders, there are several good reasons to leave office. It may be that their mission is truly accomplished. Key objectives have been achieved, and now it is time for another challenge. For other self-aware leaders, it may be time to admit the passion is no longer there. Their interest may have waned. In rarer circumstances, the leader may be ill, or too old to function effectively. Nothing is sadder than a sick leader trying to hold on to office while too ill to do the position justice.

It is a tragedy that more leaders do not recognize when it is time to go. Some leaders' wonderful careers are marred at the very end by being forced out or fired. If only leaders had a magic mirror to tell them when it is time to leave with grace and dignity. This is where a trusted advisor can make a real difference, delivering the truth in a way that helps the leader do the right thing.

What about getting fired? No successor involvement. No positive communication coming from the organization. Even in this circumstance, the exiting leader still has the opportunity to create a positive last impression. Exiting with grace and dignity, even after being fired, is the mark of a truly masterful leader; one destined to succeed elsewhere.

Dignified Departure

After five years of success, a CEO was fired by the board chair. The CEO did not see his firing coming, but he should have. Two years previous to the firing, the CEO hired the board chair's son into a senior executive position, against the advice of his own vice presidents and his trusted outside advisor. The new vice president undermined the CEO from day one. When the CEO was fired, the board chair immediately installed his son as CEO—no search necessary. The fired CEO exited with grace and dignity and had the last laugh. He went on to a new CEO job in a much nicer community in a hospital twice as large as the one he left. He then led his new hospital to its most successful decade in its 100-year history. Succeeding was this CEO's best revenge.

Chapter 46: Succession

One of the hardest decisions a leader makes is arranging for his own succession. Many leaders do not make this decision easily. They wait too long and have succession forced upon them. Masterful leaders recognize when their time has come and plan for succession.

It is time for a leader to go when any of these themes are present:

- Makes excuses for declining organization performance instead of making plans to improve performance.
- Spends more time living in the past than planning for the future.
- Becomes fixated on his exit deal.
- Falls asleep during meetings.
- Is angry when answering the phone before learning who is calling.

1. **Prepare for succession.**

2. **Never hang on by your fingernails.**

3. **Don't critique your successor.**

Recognizing these themes takes situational awareness. Recognize when it is time to go and have the insight to plan for a gracious exit from the organization. Never telegraph too far in advance your plans to step down. Six to twelve months notice to the organization is sufficient time to arrange for a successor and pass the torch to the incoming leader.

Always have a succession plan in place. Always leave at least one highly capable leader who can assume the leadership reins. It is up to the organization to select the successor, but the departing leader should always give the organization a good choice. When a successor is selected and a timeframe decided upon, the exiting leader has a wonderful opportunity to communicate positively about the successor and to thank the organization for the opportunity to serve. The leader's exit will form a lasting last impression.

After the new leader is selected, exit graciously and expeditiously. Masterful leaders offer counsel and advice to the new leader, but don't press unsolicited advice. Prepare the way for the successor by making positive comments to direct report subordinates and the staff and physicians who will report to the new leader. Never second-guess your successor, either publicly or privately.

Sleeping Beauty

One historically successful CEO was clinging to office, even though he must have known his time had come. He had had a successful 30-year career, and his current CEO tenure went well for more than a decade. As he passed normal retirement age, he lost his passion and his energy. He rarely made it through meetings, including his own board meetings, without falling asleep. No one wanted to tell him to step down. He hired two COOs; in both cases the intent was for the COO to be his successor. The first COO got tired of waiting and left after three years. The second COO started looking for a new job after a two-year wait for the CEO's retirement party. This CEO could not face reality, leaving his organization's future uncertain.

THE MEANING OF MASTERFUL LEADERSHIP

Some leaders are poor performers. Most are average. A few are great. At the pinnacle are masterful leaders. Leaders become masterful, they do not start out masterful. They listen. They learn throughout their careers. They have character and unshakable integrity. They mentor and encourage others to do their best. Masterful leaders inspire people. They are wonderful teachers. They improve lives and leave behind organizations and people far better for their presence.

Chapter 47: What Masterful Leaders Never Do

No leader is perfect, even a masterful leader. However, there are certain behaviors that masterful leaders avoid at all costs. Among those behaviors are:

- Dishonesty.
- Berating subordinates in public settings.
- Losing their temper and showing anger.
- Interrupting meetings to answer e-mails or text messages.
- Setting a poor example in any context.
- Isolation from patients and staff.
- Tolerating poor behavior in subordinates.
- Saying one thing; doing another.
- Acting so inconsistently subordinates need an interpreter.

There are certainly other bad behaviors, but this list contains key behaviors to be avoided on the journey to becoming a masterful leader. Every leader has bad moments and bad days. No one is perfect. But masterful leaders are disciplined enough that bad moments become learning experiences and are few and far between.

1. **Never tolerate dishonesty.**

2. **Never accept poor behavior.**

3. **Learn from mistakes.**

If one bad behavior were to be selected as unforgivable, it would be dishonesty. If a leader is dishonest or he tolerates dishonesty anywhere in the organization, there is no way that leader will ever be masterful, no matter how many other positive characteristics he may possess. You cannot live above your character.

Chapter 48: Defining Moments

In a thirty-five year career, there are 18.4 million moments. Some of these are defining moments. Defining moments are profoundly important situations where choices present themselves for a decision. The outcome of the decision can change the course of a life, or a career, or an enterprise.

Many kinds of defining moments present themselves in a career. The most consistently encountered are people-defining moments: a hiring decision; a firing decision; a choice of who to promote or who to mentor as a successor.

1. **Be ready for defining moments.**

2. **Use your moral compass to recognize the right thing.**

3. **Always do the right thing.**

There are strategic defining moments too. These are choices that make or break a healthcare enterprise. Whether to acquire another hospital, a physician practice, or a leading-edge clinical technology. Make the right choice and the enterprise flourishes. Make the wrong choice, and the enterprise withers and perhaps dies.

There are patient care defining moments. One choice may lead to correcting a medical error or apologizing for a serious customer service mishap. Another choice may be to recruit a new medical specialist with exceptional expertise. Another choice may be to eliminate a clinical service because a competing hospital does it better. Make the right choice and better patient care follows. The wrong choice may harm a patient or deny him the best treatment option.

Then there are integrity defining moments. Making the right choice, the choice with integrity, may temporarily harm a career. It may cause financial losses. It may cause personal or organizational embarrassment. At an integrity defining moment, the leader is challenged in a profound way. There are no websites or books for guidance during these moments. "Defining Moments" is not a graduate school class. When these moments present themselves, there is only situational awareness and moral compass readings and a clear sense of right and wrong.

Defining moments are lonely. The leader must make choices, knowing the consequences may be grave. Masterful leaders never flinch at these moments. They know behind every grave consequence lies great opportunity. Masterful leaders do not run from defining moments. They run toward them.

Chapter 49: Measures of Success

How does a masterful leader measure success? There are numerous good answers to this question. Many leaders point to improved financial performance as their preferred measure of success. Growth in revenue, improvements in profitability, upgraded bond ratings, increases in the healthcare organization's net worth--all are excellent measures of financial success and many leaders can lay claim to successful careers based on these metrics.

1. **Lead people well.**

2. **Set a personal example.**

3. **Change lives for the better.**

Improvements in quality metrics are also excellent measures of a leader's success, as are improvements in customer satisfaction. Gains in market share and community perception are also measures of success. And then there are improvements in morale. Physician and employee morale improvements stem from culture improvements, which emanate from the organization's leader. All of these metrics together define leadership success.

There are other measures, too. Improving the quality of governance is a legacy of many CEOs because they transcend the CEO's tenure. Improvement in leadership quality is another profoundly important measure of a leader's success. A leader who develops his team's talents leaves behind a strong organization that will continue to thrive long after he has gone. A good leader leaves behind a competent staff. A masterful leader leaves behind a successor and a team of leaders, some of whom will someday become successful CEOs.

Masterful healthcare leaders improve their organizations and the quality of life in the communities they serve. The most gratifying measure of success is the knowledge that masterful leadership changes lives for the better.

Flight of a Lifetime

I had been appointed as a new CEO for a struggling community hospital with a horrible reputation. Market research showed that the state's University Hospital had the best reputation for quality in our region. With the blessing and strong support of board and physician leaders, I convinced the University Hospital's leadership to create an affiliation arrangement, the first of its kind in the state, so that our hospital could access the physicians and clinical services of this stellar organization. One new service was the transport helicopter for critically ill patients.

Not long after the affiliation papers were signed to much local fanfare with the governor presiding, an expectant mother and her husband pulled off the nearby interstate and rushed to our emergency room. She delivered a very premature infant whose viability was much in question. The University Hospital helicopter flew to pick up mother and newborn. I was at the helipad to watch them depart. The obstetrician and pediatrician who assisted in the emergency delivery were at my side. One of them said, as the helicopter lifted off, "That baby has a chance. Without our new affiliation and helicopter, that baby would be gone by now."

The baby made it, thanks to the flight crew, the specialist nurses and physicians on board the helicopter, and the University Hospital team. Our leadership decision to pursue the affiliation saved a life that day.

Chapter 50: What Masterful Leaders Always Do

"Leadership is a potent combination of strategy and character. But if you must be without one, be without strategy."   Gen. H. Norman Schwarzkopf

The best leaders constantly exhibit certain positive traits. Together, these traits define greatness. Masterful leaders always endeavor to:

- Follow a true moral compass with character.
- Be good listeners.
- Connect with staff, physicians, and patients.
- Show a touch of humanity.
- Differentiate outcomes from efforts.
- Make decisions and don't look back.
- Truthfully evaluate direct reports.
- Fire ineffective people.
- Demonstrate grace and dignity when taking and leaving office.
- Encourage direct reports to be truthful, even if it hurts.
- Have courage.
- Measure success in terms of lives positively influenced.

1. **Be a good listener.**

2. **Always speak the truth.**

3. **Show a touch of humanity often.**

Masterful leaders are made, not born. The bond between leaders and character becomes stronger with time, experience, and wisdom gained. In early years of a career, the bond is like rubber cement. As leaders grow and mature, the bond grows stronger, like Gorilla Glue. As leaders reach their pinnacle and become masterful, the bond between leaders and character is like epoxy, enormously strong and unbreakable.

Healthcare masterful leaders are abundant. They are department directors, physician chairs, vice presidents, nursing supervisors, CEOs, and many more. Masterful leaders and their organizations achieve success, no matter the organization's size, finances, or competitive challenges. They inspire leaders of the future by their positive example, mentoring, and teaching.

If one attribute were selected as the most important for masterful leadership, it would be character. Masterful leaders are everywhere. Aspire to become one.